The Whole Grain Diet Miracle

The Whole Grain Diet Miracle

THE HEALTHIEST DIET EVER!

Lisa Hark, Ph.D, RD
University of Pennsylvania
School of Medicine

Darwin Deen, MD, MS
Albert Einstein College
of Medicine

Dedications

Dr. Lisa Hark: To my loving children, Jamie (11) and Brett (7). They're a healthy, whole-grain eating crew and I love them very much.

To my parents, Diane and Jerry, for their ongoing love and support no matter how many new challenges come my way. To my brothers and their families David, Cinde, and Nicholas; Jeffrey, Stacy, Rachel, Louis, and Joel; and Richard, Pam, Alexandra, Mitchell, and Samantha for all their love and friendship.

Finally to Darwin, for helping me to realize my dreams. I am proud to continue working together.

Dr. Darwin Deen: To my mom, who introduced me to the healthy good taste of whole-wheat bread when I was 6 years old, at a time when our local supermarket did not carry it, and from whom I got my interest in nutrition.

To my sons, Ben (18) and Jesse (15), and all my patients' children who I hope will recognize the importance of whole grains and eat healthy their whole lives.

DK

London, New York, Munich, Melbourne, and Delhi

Senior Editor Anja Schmidt
Art Director Dirk Kaufman
Designer Timothy Shaner
DTP Coordinator Kathy Farias
Production Manager Ivor Parker
Executive Managing Editor Sharon Lucas
Publisher Carl Raymond

Published by DK Publishing, Inc., 375 Hudson Street, New York, New York 10014

06 07 08 09 10 9 8 7 6 5 4 3 2 1

A catalog record for this book is available from the Library of Congress.

ISBN 0-7566-2058-9

Printed and bound in USA by R. R. Donnelley & Sons

Discover more at
www.dk.com

Contents

Preface

Why this book? As a doctor and a nutritionist, we are very convinced by the overwhelmingly positive scientific research that shows that eating whole grains on a daily basis can help you to lose weight, fight chronic diseases, and live longer. We are compelled to share these benefits by writing *The Whole Grain Diet Miracle*, which includes 50 easy and delicious whole grain recipes and a 6-week weight loss menu.

Why a miracle? We have dedicated our careers to educating physicians and patients about the science of nutrition, and much of our efforts are devoted to clearing up the confusion about fad diets, because they are rarely based on real science. The reality is that as two health professionals we never expected to collaborate on a diet book. But when it comes to whole grains, we realized that with over 80 scientific studies supporting their benefits, we needed to get the word out. Because so few things in nutrition science are certain, this seems like a miracle to us, hence, the title *The Whole Grain Diet Miracle*.

Why now? Grains have been cultivated for thousands of years, but food processing seriously diminishes their value. The American diet has become increasingly based on processed food and, as a society, we need to get back to eating foods in their natural state if we expect to improve our health and live longer. Our message is simple and scientifically supported, which makes it ideal for a realistic and easy-to-follow diet book.

What to expect? *The Whole Grain Diet Miracle* will help you change your eating habits and improve your long-term health. In it, we describe the history, nutritional value, and health benefits of the most popular whole grains. Our goal is to help you understand whole grains' effects on body weight, satiety, blood sugar, cholesterol levels, and on the gastrointestinal tract. Eating more whole grains will no doubt improve your health and, although this is a diet book, it is really meant to be a new way of eating for the rest of your life. Even those who are allergic to wheat can enjoy the benefits of eating other whole grains. We promise that if you follow the menus and incorporate the recipes into your daily schedule and exercise regularly, you will have more energy, feel better, look better, and live longer.

What's the bottom line? Whole grains are now widely available in supermarkets, specialty stores, health food stores, and even on the Internet. So read this book, have fun stocking your pantry with whole grains, and start this program now. Working whole grains into your diet is easier and more delicious than you ever imagined!

LISA A. HARK, PH.D, RD
University of Pennsylvania
School of Medicine, Philadelphia

DARWIN DEEN, MD, MS
Albert Einstein College
of Medicine, New York

Whole grains are the form of the grain as it exists in **nature**.

The Miracle

The *Whole Grain Diet Miracle* really is a miracle. For the first time in history, we can prescribe a weight-loss diet that has a tremendous amount of scientifically proven health benefits. We are advising, with a great deal of certainty, that eating more whole grains in their natural form will help you not only to control your weight, but also to reduce your risk of heart disease, diabetes, stroke, and colon cancer as well as to lower your blood pressure and cholesterol levels. Eating more whole grains has been shown to save lives and reduce death rates. So what are you waiting for? It's easier than you think.

The Whole Grain Diet Miracle provides you with a step-by-step approach to buying, storing, cooking, and eating whole grains. We describe common grains (wheat, rye, oats, barley, bulgur, corn, buckwheat, and quinoa) and not-so-common grains (amaranth, spelt, sorghum, teff, triticale, and farro). We highlight each grain's nourishing powers and teach you how to make whole grains an integral part of your healthy lifestyle. We provide six weeks of menus and 50 recipes. With all this excitement about eating whole grains, lots of questions arise about how to incorporate them into our everyday diets, and we do our best to answer them.

GETTING TO KNOW WHOLE GRAINS

What are whole grains?

Whole grains are the form of the grain as it exists in nature. Generally unprocessed or minimally processed, a whole grain consists of the entire seed of the plant, which consists of the bran, endosperm, and the germ.

The bran, or the multilayer outer skin, is primarily for protection. It provides the majority of the grain's fiber, and also B vitamins, minerals, trace elements, antioxidants, and phytochemicals.

The endosperm, or middle layer, is the largest portion of the grain or seed and is the source of protein, carbohydrates, and some vitamins. The endosperm provides the germ with a constant supply of energy, allowing the plant to grow roots for water absorption and sprouts to capture sunlight.

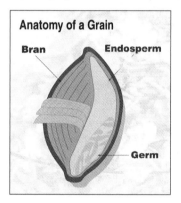

The germ, or inner layer, is a rich source of vitamins, trace minerals, unsaturated fats, phytochemicals, and antioxidants, which are different from those found in fruits and vegetables and unique to whole grains. The germ enables the seed to form a new plant when sowed.

What are the functions of these vitamins and minerals?

THIAMIN, also known as vitamin B_1, helps the body convert carbohydrates and fats into energy. It is essential for normal growth and development and helps to maintain proper functioning of the heart, nervous system, and digestive system.

RIBOFLAVIN, also known as vitamin B_2, is necessary for the release of energy from carbohydrates, is needed for normal growth and development, and helps to build up glucose molecules into the complex carbohydrate glycogen, which is stored in the liver and muscles for future use. Riboflavin helps digest fats; helps protect the nervous system; and also maintains mucous membranes.

NIACIN, also known as vitamin B_3, nicotinic acid, or niacinamide, participates in at least 200 different chemical reactions involved in energy release. It is also necessary for the production and breakdown of glucose, fats, and amino acids; the development, maintenance, and function of the skin, stomach, intestines, and nervous system; and in manufacturing DNA (the substance that makes up our genes).

FOLATE is a B vitamin that plays an essential role in tissue growth and development, including a central role in making DNA and RNA (the substances needed to make proteins). It works with vitamin B_{12} to form hemoglobin for red blood cells. Folate reduces the risk of a fetus developing a neural tube defect, and may reduce the risk of heart disease by helping to lower blood homocysteine levels.

IRON is an essential mineral in all cells of the body. It is a component of hemoglobin (the oxygen-carrying protein in red blood cells) and myoglobin (a protein found in muscle cells) and is involved in the release of energy from glucose and fatty acids.

PHOSPHORUS is an essential mineral present in bones and teeth. It is a constituent of lipids, proteins, carbohydrates, enzymes, and DNA, and is present in ATP, a compound that stores the energy used by all cells. When combined with oxygen as phosphate, it helps to maintain the body's normal pH levels and normal cell membrane structure.

CALCIUM, an important mineral, plays an essential role in normal bone mineralization; maintenance of cell membrane permeability; normal muscle contractions and nervous system contractions; and normal blood clotting. Ninety percent of the body's calcium is found in the bones.

MAGNESIUM, another important mineral, plays a vital role in the formation of bones and teeth. Magnesium works with many vitamins for their proper enzyme function and is essential for smooth muscle relaxation, which is vitally important in regulating heart beat and circulation.

COPPER, a mineral, plays a key role in several body functions including the production of skin, hair, and eye pigment; the development of healthy bones, teeth, and heart; the protection of body cells from chemical damage, since it acts as an antioxidant; the maintenance of the myelin sheath, which surrounds and protects nerve fibers; and the functioning of the nervous system. It is also involved in the processing of iron in the body and the formation of red blood cells.

MANGANESE is a trace mineral that is a component of several enzymes, which help to break down carbohydrates, proteins, and fats. It helps activate enzymes that stimulate formation of cartilage in skin and bone. Manganese is also thought to be of importance in brain function.

SELENIUM is an antioxidant and part of an enzyme that protects cells from the damaging effects of free radicals, which can lead to heart disease. It is also thought to have anticancer properties. Selenium is vital for the immune system and the thyroid gland.

What are the benefits of antioxidants and phytochemicals?

Antioxidants are substances naturally occurring in foods that help neutralize the damaging effects of free radicals, which occur as by-products of normal metabolic processes. If the body's supply of antioxidants is insufficient to prevent cell and tissue damage, the risk of developing heart disease and cancer, can increase. Sources of antioxidants include vitamins A, C, and E, and the minerals copper, selenium, and zinc. Whole grains contain a variety of unique antioxidants. For example, oats contain avenanthramide, antioxidants that help reduce free-radical damage to LDL cholesterol (the bad kind), thus reducing the risk of cardiovascular disease.

Phytochemicals are natural substances produced by plants to protect the plant from viruses and bacteria. They are also believed to benefit the human immune system, defending it against heart disease, cancer, and diabetes. The best way to get phytochemicals in the diet is from natural, unprocessed foods, such as whole grains, beans, fruits, and vegetables. The bran and germ portions of the whole grain provide a particularly rich source of phytochemicals.

The **germ**, or inner layer, enables the seed to form a new plant when sowed and is a rich source of **vitamins**, trace minerals, unsaturated fats, phytochemicals, and **antioxidants**.

Can't I just take a vitamin or mineral supplement?

Scientist have devoted millions of dollars and thousands of hours of research over the last 25 years trying to reproduce the health benefits from whole grains by supplementing humans, as well as animals, with fiber, vitamins, minerals, and even antioxidants and phytochemicals. Most of these studies have been disappointing, proving that when it comes to nutrition, the whole is truly greater than the sum of its parts. So no, you can't get the benefits of whole grains by taking a supplement. There is no substitute for eating whole grains on a regular basis.

How are grains refined?

Refined grains are stripped of the bran and germ during the milling process — usually to make white flour — leaving only the endosperm portion behind. Without the bran and the germ, there is very little fiber. Refining also reduces the protein content by 25% and removes 17 key nutrients, including about 66% of the B vitamins and 70% of the minerals. Most of the phytochemicals and antioxidants are also removed, all of which make these products unhealthy choices. However, because refining increases a product's shelf-life, it is favored by the food industry. Foods made from refined grains often list ingredients such as bleached, unbleached, white, or enriched flour, which are used to make white bread, cakes, muffins, rolls, breadsticks, crackers, cookies, and pasta.

Although manufacturers enrich or fortify most refined foods with some of the missing nutrients, fortification does not make up for the vast stores of lost vitamins, minerals, and fiber content. Other than iron, most minerals are not replaced. In addition, the whole-grain components (germ, endosperm, and bran) seem to work together as a unit rather than separately after they are refined.

Why are whole grains so good for you?

Whole grains in their natural form are a rich source of fiber, vitamins, minerals, antioxidants, and phytochemicals. In fact, the scientific evidence supporting whole grains in the diet is strong enough that the FDA has approved a health claim on labels stating, *"Diets rich in whole grain foods and other plant foods, and low in saturated fat and cholesterol, may help reduce the risk of heart disease and certain cancers."* Foods containing 51% or more whole grains can use this health claim to identify their products as healthy.

Numerous studies have also shown that eating more whole grains can help control your weight and reduce your risk of heart disease, stroke, diabetes, and cancer. These benefits are most likely due to a reduction in blood pressure and cholesterol, as well as improved insulin resistance. Eating more whole grains has been shown to save lives as well.

Whole grains may decrease hunger by making you feel full and by curbing blood-sugar spikes that trigger appetite. We describe many of the studies supporting these claims in Chapter 1.

How much do I need to eat to experience these benefits?

Because of all the health benefits, the 2005 US Dietary Guidelines advise Americans to eat three to five servings of whole grains every day. (One serving is one ounce or one slice of whole-grain bread). Most Americans eat less than one serving daily, and about a third of us don't eat any at all. Our six-week daily menus provide 42 days of ideas to guide you in choosing at least three servings of whole grains every day. Since incorporating more whole grains into your diet should be a gradual process, we describe how to make the transition on page 121. We also cross-reference these menus to 50 delicious recipes, many of which are quick and easy to make.

How can I distinguish between whole grains and fiber?

It is important to note that just because a food is high in fiber, does not necessarily make it a good source of whole grains. In fact, whole-grain foods vary in fiber content, as shown in the nutritional charts within each grain's description. Therefore, looking at fiber alone may not help you determine whether the food is indeed a good source of whole grain.

Whole-grain cereals, such as shredded wheat, have less fiber than bran cereals because bran cereals have the hull of the wheat kernel added in extra amounts (more than was present in the whole grain).

What is the difference between soluble and insoluble fiber?

Whole grains are rich in soluble and insoluble fiber, both of which are important for maintaining a healthy digestive system. Soluble fiber is found in foods such as oatmeal, barley, rye, beans, legumes, and citrus fruits. This type of fiber slows the breakdown and absorption of sugar, possibly leading to reduced levels of sugar in the blood. This may explain why there is a reduced risk of developing diabetes in people who eat whole grains on a daily basis. During digestion, soluble fiber forms a gel-like substance that binds bile acids, which are needed for cholesterol absorption. If eaten in sufficient quantities, this type of fiber can help reduce the quantity of cholesterol in the blood, which may explain why eating whole grains reduces the risk of developing heart disease.

Insoluble fiber is found in wheat bran, whole-wheat products like breads and cereals, popcorn, brown rice, and leafy vegetables. This type of fiber does not dissolve easily in water and is not digested or absorbed by the body. However, its presence in the diet helps keep the gastrointestinal tract clear and promotes regular bowel movements. Therefore, eating more insoluble fiber may be protective against colon cancer as well as helping to prevent constipation, hemorrhoids, and diverticulosis—the presence of small pouches (know as diverticuli) in the wall of the colon, which occur when part of the intestine bulges outward through weak areas (see page 43 for more information).

Can I still eat whole grains if I am allergic to wheat?

If your doctor has diagnosed you with celiac disease and requires you to eliminate gluten from your diet, the grains you should stay away from include all types of wheat (cracked, bulgur, durum, spelt, couscous, kamut) as well as oats, rye, and barley. Be careful when inspecting ingredient lists for the presence of gluten: unless a grain product specifically says it is gluten-free, it should be assumed that gluten is present. Depending on

Eating more whole **grains** has actually been shown to **save lives** as well. Whole grains may **decrease hunger** by making you feel full and by curbing **blood sugar** spikes that trigger the **appetite**.

your symptoms, it may be necessary to eliminate completely or just partially eliminate these specific grains from your diet. Talk to your doctor about specific dietary needs and consult your physician before making any dietary changes.

There is no reason to eliminate all whole grains even if you have a wheat allergy, because there are many nutrient-dense, high-fiber whole grains that are naturally gluten-free. For example, rice, buckwheat, amaranth, corn, and quinoa do not contain any gluten. Look for products made from these gluten-free grains, such as flour, pancake mix, baked goods, and cereals, to replace those made from wheat. In addition, many of our recipes incorporate gluten-free grains into everything from appetizers to desserts. (See page 45 for more information.)

Will eating grains cause bloating or increased gas production?

It is important to introduce whole grains into your diet gradually so that your body has a chance to adjust, and we describe how to transition your diet on page 121. When we eat, our bodies digest food by breaking it down into the simpler forms so that it can be more easily absorbed. Whole grains contain "indigestable" carbohydrate, commonly referred to as fiber, that cannot be broken down into sugars in the small intestine where they would be absorbed. Instead these complex carbohydrates travel to the large intestine where they are broken down by normal gut bacteria into short chain fatty acids, which may be responsible for some of the important health benefits of fiber (see page 39). These gut bacteria are the actual "gas producers," so whenever you add more fiber to your diet, there is a period of adjustment needed to feel comfortable with this change in gas production. This is perfectly normal. If you experience more gas than you would like, Beano® is a dietary supplement that contains the galactosidase enzyme from a natural source and helps your body break down these foods, making them more digestible.

FINDING WHOLE GRAINS

How can I identify whole grains in foods?

In January 2005, *The Wall Street Journal* cited whole grains as the "new darling" of the food industry, and consumer interest in products labeled with "whole grains" is growing. Food manufacturers are speeding up production of whole-grain cereals, breads, pasta, cookies, bagels, tortillas, couscous, and even frozen dinners to meet consumer demand. However, sorting out which products truly contain whole grains can be confusing. Here are some tips that will make your search easier and ensure that you are getting the best sources of whole grains.

■ Aim for 100% whole grain as the first ingredient. The best sources of whole grains are whole grains themselves. Sold in packages or found in self-serve bins, grains such as wheat berries, bulgur, quinoa, millet, amaranth, brown rice, and oats.

■ When reading the ingredients, look for the word "whole" in front of the type of grain. Again, ideally this item should be first on the ingredient list. For example, whole barley, whole oats, cracked wheat, and whole cornmeal. If the grain is listed as the second ingredient, it could make up only 1% to 49% of the product.

■ Look for products carrying an FDA-approved health claim that attests to their whole-grain ingredients. If the product has over 51% whole grain, it is allowed by law to state: *"Diets rich in whole grain foods and other plant foods, and low in total fat, saturated fat, and cholesterol, may reduce the risk of heart disease and certain cancers."*

■ Don't trust a food's color to determine whether it is made from whole grains. Foods that are dark or brown in color are often associated with whole grains, but their appearance may instead result from artificial food colorings or other added ingredients, such as molasses. Similarly, healthful whole-grain foods made with oats and amaranth can be light in color.

■ When purchasing breakfast cereals, look for those with greater than 5 grams of fiber per serving and with less than 4 grams of sugar per serving. Because fruit naturally contains sugar, some cereals that contain fruit, such as raisin bran, will list over 10 grams of sugar on the label. However, this is still a good source of whole grains.

What about the Whole Grain Council's stamp on food products?

It is easy to be confused by food labels and, with more and more new products coming on the market, things are only going to get more complicated. Beginning in 2005, the Whole Grains Council launched an official Whole Grain Stamp to help consumers identify whole grain products more easily. According to the USDA's 2005 Dietary Guidelines, three servings of whole grains translates into 48 grams of whole grains per day. The Whole Grain Council has developed three stamps to help consumers meet this goal. Foods labeled as a "Good Source" of whole grains contain at least 8 grams of whole grains. An "Excellent Source" contains at least 16 grams of whole grains. A "100% Excellent Source" contains at least 16 grams of whole grain and guarantees that all grain ingredients contained in the product are from whole grains.

What about other grain ingredients listed on labels?

A product labeled "multigrain" may not necessarily contain whole grain—all the word "multigrain" tells you is that the product contains different grains mixed together, not necessarily whole grains (they may be refined). Phrases such as "100% rye" typically mean that rye is the only grain in the product—this does not guarantee that the rye is

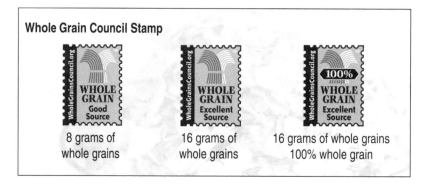

Whole Grain Council Stamp

8 grams of whole grains

16 grams of whole grains

16 grams of whole grains 100% whole grain

whole-grain. Check the ingredients for the words "whole rye." The term "stoneground," which is a technique for grinding grains, does not ensure that the grain remains whole. Usually, stoneground grains retain the germ, but not the bran, so they are not truly whole grains. In such cases, refined flour, not whole-grain flour, usually appears first on the ingredient list. Similarly, packages labeled "bran," "seven grain," or "pumpernickel" are filled with a variety of grains, but they may actually contain little or no whole grains. As always, be sure to check the ingredient list.

What about selecting and storing whole grains?

In the past you would have had to travel to a health-food store to find whole grains, but now many supermarkets carry brands such as Arrowhead Mills and Bob's Red Mill, and many other companies are developing whole-grain products. Since grains contain oils that may turn rancid over time, it's best to buy only what you think you will use in the next few months. Grains are usually found prepacked in your local supermarket or in bulk bins in health food stores. Before you purchase from bulk bins, make sure the store has a good turnover to ensure freshness. Check to see that the bins are securely covered and that the grains are free of debris and moisture. Smelling is also a good way of determining whether grains are fresh. They should not have a rancid odor. Oats have a slightly higher fat content than other grains and may turn rancid more quickly. (See page 50 for storing information.)

Do I need to buy any special equipment to cook whole grains?

All you will need to prepare our simple, whole-grain recipes and quick meals is a stove, standard pots, and water. If you are motivated to bake breads, you may consider using a bread machine, but this is not critical. Other appliances that you may already own can also come in handy, such as a food processor, grinder, or mortar and pestle. Since more and more companies are producing a variety of whole grain flours, using a flour mill will probably not be necessary.

Chapter 1
Health Benefits

The Scientific Evidence

The *Whole Grain Diet* is a miracle because it shows you how to lose weight while increasing your intake of the very foods that nutrition science have demonstrated time and time again are the healthiest for you to eat. Surprisingly, this approach runs contrary to many of the most popular diets of the last decade.

Over the last 30 years, researchers have documented the benefits of whole grains in study after study. Starting in 1972, with a groundbreaking paper by Dr. Hugh Trowell, research has shown that diets high in fiber and whole grains were protective against heart disease. The next year he extended his theory to show that whole grains also helped protect against diabetes. Since that time, scientists have added to the evidence that eating a diet rich in whole grains is linked to a reduced risk of cardiovascular disease, diabetes, insulin resistance (a precursor to diabetes), obesity, and premature death. Due to the quantity of research data, the US Food and Drug Administration in 1999 approved a health claim for foods containing whole grains that states: *"Diets rich in whole-grain foods and other plant foods and low in total fat, saturated fat, and cholesterol may reduce the risk for heart disease and certain cancers."*

Popular diets all recommend reducing or eliminating entire food groups, even though these foods contain important nutrients. High-protein, low-carbohydrate diets have been the latest rage, and whole grains are often eliminated or restricted, since they are high in carbohydrates. However, while these popular diets ban carbohydrates, scientists have been compiling study after study documenting the importance of whole grains for a healthy diet. In addition, the USDA's Food Guide Pyramid continued to advocate that carbohydrate-rich foods should form the foundation of a healthy diet. Did all of these nutrition experts really get it wrong?

Supporters of low-carbohydrate diets have charged that the Food Guide Pyramid is responsible for the epidemic of obesity in the United States. However, research shows that the problem more likely stems from eating too many calories (our portion sizes are the largest in the world) and too many refined carbohydrates, such as sugar, corn syrup, and baked goods made with refined and processed grains.

Evidence shows that you can lose weight without eliminating carbohydrates—in other words, you don't have to make yourself unhealthy to get thinner. Vegetarians, for example, who eat mostly whole grains, legumes (beans), fruits, and vegetables have very low rates of heart disease, cancer, and diabetes. In our opinion, it's all about choosing the right foods—foods that have been shown over and over again to dominate the diets of the healthiest people in the world.

In this section we provide an overview of many studies over the last 30 years that document the important benefits of whole grains in preventing chronic disease. As you read this section, consider your own medical issues and your parents, and grandparents, health as well. If you have a family history of any of the medical problems we address, then incorporating more whole grains into your diet is especially important.

Promotes Weight Loss

Over the past 10 years numerous studies have documented the relationship between whole grain intake and reduced risk of obesity. If you compare diets from different countries, those with the highest fiber consumption have the lowest rates of obesity. Within the US population, fiber intake and breakfast intake have each been shown to be associated with a lower body mass index level (BMI; the ratio of your weight to your height). The reasons for this association are complex but worth considering.

Less Hunger

■ Whole grains are higher in protein than refined grains, and high-protein diets can reduce hunger. People who eat whole grains may eat less, and that may be part of the reason they weigh less.

■ Another part of the explanation may lie in the fact that many whole grains are excellent sources of fiber, and studies have shown that high fiber intake is also associated with less hunger. Whole grains contain starches that are digested more slowly, resulting in a lower blood-glucose concentration and insulin level compared to those eating refined carbohydrates. (This important effect is discussed further in the section on Diabetes, page 32.) Lower levels of insulin mean that less fat is stored and you are less hungry at your next meal.

■ Studies have also demonstrated that if you eat whole grains for breakfast, you will eat less food at lunch and dinner. In fact, one study shows that a cereal and milk meal twice a day with a healthy lunch is as effective for weight loss as taking a meal replacement shake (and most of us feel much less hungry after a bowl of cereal than after a shake). According to the US National Weight Control Registry, an ongoing study of more than 4,000 people who have lost weight and kept it off, 80% of these successful dieters eat breakfast. So, if you're not a breakfast eater, it's time to start. If you are, consider breakfast as an ideal opportunity to add whole grains to your diet.

Calories and Low-Fat Diets

The "caloric density" of whole grains is low. That means that you can eat more of them and feel less hungry, while at the same time, taking fewer calories in. Caloric density of a food is determined by its fat, fiber, and water content. Whole grains are high in fiber and low in fat and therefore have a low caloric density. Many studies designed to evaluate the effects of altering caloric density have shown that lower caloric density diets are associated with improved satiety (feeling full) and with reduced calorie intake.

In the ongoing Health Professionals Follow-up Study conducted by researchers at the Harvard School of Public Health of more than 40,000 men who were not trying to lose weight, the more whole grains eaten by the participants, the lower their weight gain over time. In fact, after eight years, weight was about one pound lower for every 40 grams of whole grains eaten each day.

In a review of the existing scientific research on dietary energy density and weight regulation published in the journal *Nutrition Reviews* in 2001, the authors concluded, "the longer people followed a low energy dense diet, the better it worked," and suggested that the best way to lower the energy density of your diet is to increase fiber and decrease fat. These researchers combined the results of 12 different studies to show that more weight is lost on a diet that is high in fiber and low in fat than on a diet that is only low in fat. This may be because low-fat diets are not very "filling," and that adding fiber restores the diets' "satiety" (ability to make you feel full).

Examining data from the ongoing Nurses Health Study of 90,600 women, Simin Liu and colleagues from the Harvard School of Public Health concluded that "women who consumed more whole grains consistently weighed less than women who consumed less."

In one of the few studies looking at children, L. Steffen and colleagues at the University of Minnesota documented in 2003 a lower BMI and greater insulin sensitivity among adolescents who ate more whole grains (see Diabetes section for a discussion of insulin sensitivity on page 33).

The Bottom Line: Weight Control

Recent studies comparing different weight-loss diets (such as Atkins, the Zone, and Weight Watchers) have shown that while each of these diets can help people to lose weight successfully in the short run, all of them are associated with regain of most of the lost weight since most people eventually tire of the diet and go back to their usual intake. For this reason, long-term weight control rather than short-term weight loss is what is ultimately important.

Whole grains represent a logical (because they are healthy) and effective way to control your weight in the long term. The weight that you lose on a whole-grain diet will be kept off because this diet works better the longer you follow it.

Heart Disease

More than 70 million people in the United States suffer from some form of heart disease. In all its various forms, heart disease is the number one cause of premature death in America. No other disease is as widespread. In 2002, more than 900,000 individuals died from some form of heart disease. That's over 2,500 deaths per day, or an average of one death every 34 seconds. Caring for people with heart disease costs an estimated $400 billion a year.

During the last 20 years, increased public awareness of the role of diet and exercise, improved screening and early detection of heart disease, and more aggressive treatment of risk factors, such as high blood pressure and high cholesterol, have led to a decline in the number of deaths from these diseases.

Risk Factors for Heart Disease

Many factors are known to increase your risk of developing heart disease; some you cannot control, others you can, as shown on page 30.

Your age, gender, family history, and genetic makeup cannot be altered, but you can reduce their impact with proper diet and exercise. By adopting a healthier lifestyle, which includes eating healthy every day, controlling your weight and blood pressure, being physically active, and avoiding or quitting cigarette smoking, you can reduce your risk and possibly prevent heart disease.

Major Risk Factors for Heart Disease:
- Elevated LDL ("bad") cholesterol levels
- Elevated total cholesterol levels
- Low HDL ("good") cholesterol levels
- Diabetes mellitus
- Cigarette smoking and exposure to tobacco smoke
- High blood pressure
- Family history of premature heart disease (a heart attack before age 55 for men and 65 for women)
- Age (men older than 45 years; women older than 55 years)
- Obesity (BMI greater than 30)
- Sedentary lifestyle (inadequate exercise)

The Miracle Workers: Whole Grains and Heart Disease

In a 1996 study about the Health Professional's follow-up, which was published in the *Journal of the American Medical Association,* the relationship between dietary fiber intake and the risk of heart disease was described. The study found that in men, the chance of having a heart attack differed depending on how much fiber they ate every day. For the group with the highest dietary fiber intake (about 30 grams per day) the risk was nearly half that of men in the lowest group, who ate only about 12 grams per day. Importantly, cereal fiber was found to be most strongly associated with a reduced risk of a heart attack.

In a study from China, researchers found that a diet containing oats and buckwheat was linked to a lowered risk of high blood pressure and high cholesterol, respectively. Only one 3-ounce serving per day of each grain was needed to reduce blood pressure, lower total and LDL ("bad") cholesterol, and raise HDL ("good") cholesterol. One paper reporting results from the Iowa Women's Health Study, which was published in the *American Journal of Public Health* in 1999, reviewed the diets of 38,700 women between the ages of 55 and 69 years. This study found that the higher a woman's intake of whole grains, the lower her risk of heart disease. Conversely, the higher the intake of refined grains the higher the risk of heart disease.

In 2004, the *American Journal of Clinical Nutrition* reported results from M. Jensen and colleagues, who examined how much whole grain, bran, and germ would reduce the risk of heart disease. They found that the more whole grains participants ate, the lower their risk of heart disease. The reverse was also true: those who ate the least whole grains had the highest risk. The association was even stronger for bran, possibly suggesting that bran may contain the most biologically active components in the fight against cardiovascular disease.

Bottom Line: Dietary Advice

Taken together, these studies, along with many others, have clearly established the benefits of whole grains in reducing the risk of heart disease. But it is important to keep in mind that dietary saturated fat and cholesterol also need to be limited to reduce your risk of heart disease. Major sources of saturated fat and cholesterol in the diet include animal products such as fatty meats, butter, and full-fat dairy products like half and half, cheese, cream, and whole milk. Eating more fish, lean meats, and poultry, and substituting foods rich in monounsaturated fats (olive oil, canola oil, nuts, avocado), polyunsaturated fats (fish, vegetables oils, seeds, mayonnaise), and plant foods (beans, legumes, whole grains) for saturated fats, are the best dietary approaches.

Diabetes

Diabetes is defined as an abnormally high level of sugar, or glucose, in the blood. Type 1 diabetes mellitus is caused by an allergylike response within the body that damages cells in the pancreas that produce insulin, so people with Type 1 diabetes don't have the ability to produce adequate amounts of insulin. Type 1 diabetes usually starts in childhood and used to be called Juvenile Diabetes.

Type 2 diabetes, on the other hand, is associated with an overproduction of insulin, which is due to a decreased response to insulin's action in the body. Type 2 diabetes is much more common (90% of people with diabetes have Type 2) and is more likely to develop in those who are overweight or obese. While Type 2 diabetes was once referred to as Adult-Onset Diabetes, it has now been reported in children as young as 10 years of age.

According to the the American Diabetes Association, more than 1 out of every 14 Americans (7%) have diabetes and nearly one-third of them may be unaware of their condition. However, diabetes does not develop overnight. In fact, according to recent statistics, 41 million individuals, 40–74 years old, in the United States, have a condition known as "pre-diabetes." This condition can be thought of as blood glucose levels that are higher than normal, usually in the range of 100 to 125 mg/dL, but not high enough to be classified as diabetes. Before people develop Type 2 diabetes, they almost always have "pre-diabetes" or "glucose intolerance," when the body's ability to respond to carbohydrate (especially simple sugars) is impaired and "insulin resistance" develops (the body's insulin secretion is abnormal). Eventually these abnormalities lead to diabetes. Whole grains have an impact on both glucose intolerance and insulin resistance and therefore can be an important part of treatment for diabetics, as well as a means of prevention in those who have a family history of diabetes.

Fiber and Blood Sugar Control

The link between the fiber contained in whole grains and blood sugar control is not a new concept by any means. Denis Burkitt and Hugh Trowell in their landmark "fiber hypothesis," documented a relationship between diabetes and fiber intake back in the 1970s. Jim Anderson (another early proponent of the fiber hypothesis) published an article in 1979, describing how fiber exerts its important effects in the body. Since these publications, literally hundreds of scientific studies have examined the fiber hypothesis and confirmed many of the theorized benefits of fiber. The exact mechanism by which fiber affects the body is still under active investigation, but in general, these studies show a 20–40% reduced risk of diabetes in those who eat whole grains on a regular basis.

Results of the Insulin Resistance Atherosclerosis Study from 2003 demonstrated that among almost 1,000 subjects, those who ate the most whole grains had the lowest insulin levels and the greatest insulin sensitivity. Fiber was also the focus of a literature review by Venn and Mann, who concluded that "there is strong evidence to suggest that eating a variety of whole grain foods and legumes is beneficial in the prevention and management of diabetes."

Many studies show that the larger the particle size of the grain (that is, the less refined the grain), the longer it takes to digest and the slower the increase in blood glucose levels after the grain is eaten. This leads to lower insulin levels and improves (or helps maintain) insulin sensitivity. J. Montenen and colleagues from the National Public Health Institute in Helsinki, Finland, demonstrated that whole grain and cereal fiber consumption were associated with a reduced risk of diabetes, particularly Type 2. Those grains high in soluble fiber, such as oats, rye, and barley, are more effective at improving insulin sensitivity than grains high in insoluble fiber, such bulgur, wheat, and buckwheat. Other grains, such as corn and rice with minimal fiber content, did not have much of an impact on insulin sensitivity. This has led some investigators to compare the effects of various grains that contain different amounts and types of fiber.

The Miracle Workers: Whole Grains and Diabetes

M. Kabir and colleagues at the University of Paris replaced whole-wheat cereal and bread for breakfast with muesli (containing oats and fruit) and pumpernickel bread (made from rye flour) and showed that this switch from insoluble to more soluble fiber was associated with a significant decrease in both blood sugar and cholesterol levels. Another study looking at types of fiber was conducted by Wolever and colleagues at the University of Toronto. They replaced corn and rice-based cereals with wheat and oat-based cereals with added psyllium (for an even greater soluble-fiber boost) in people who had Type 2 diabetes. Then, they measured changes to short-chain fatty acids (produced by bacteria in the colon) in response to this dietary change. For the first three months very little happened, but over the next three months, there were changes in these volatile fatty acids, and along with them, reduced blood triglyceride levels and improvements in the ratio of total to HDL cholesterol levels. Their conclusion was that, over time, as these diabetic subjects adapted to a higher fiber intake, their risk of heart disease decreased.

M. Pereira and colleagues at Harvard Medical School replaced the refined grains in the diets of a group of overweight men with whole grains. They kept the calories constant to prevent weight loss (because weight loss itself causes improved insulin sensitivity) and simply replaced refined white flour with whole-wheat or oat flour. The results demonstrated that the whole grains improved insulin sensitivity. This and other studies conclude that adding fiber to the diet is indeed an important way to improve the health of people who have diabetes.

In addition to being high in fiber, whole grains are also an excellent source of magnesium, and a number of researchers believe that this mineral may also play a role in the prevention and treatment of diabetes. Using data from their large epidemiologic studies (the Health Professionals Study and the Nurses Health Study), W. Willett and colleagues at the Harvard School of Public Health identified a relationship between the intake of magnesium and the risk of developing Type 2 diabetes, which was published in *Diabetes Care* in 2004. So, at the moment, we are not sure if it is the fiber or the magnesium in whole grains that is more important in the benefits related to diabetes, but it is probably a combination of the two. While this distinction is important to scientists who seek to understand the mechanisms, we can just be happy that whole grains work, without worrying about how.

Bottom Line:
1. Diabetes risk is 25–40% lower in those with a higher whole grain intake, compared to those eating very few whole grains.
2. Higher fiber intake helps to control blood sugar in people who have already developed diabetes, potentially allowing them to use less medication and to have better control of their blood sugar levels.
3. Substituting whole grains for the refined grains in your diet will improve your insulin sensitivity, help you to lose weight, and reduce your risk of developing diabetes.

Metabolic Syndrome

Metabolic syndrome (also known as Syndrome X) is a cluster of abnormalities that combine to increase the risk of diabetes and heart disease. The components of metabolic syndrome include elevated blood pressure (even mild elevations that do not indicate hypertension are significant); increased waist circumference—more than 40 inches (100 cm) for a man or 35 inches (87½ cm) for a woman; glucose intolerance (what is also called "pre-diabetes," see page 32); elevated triglyceride levels (the most common form of fat present in the blood); and a low HDL (the "good") cholesterol level in the blood.

Currently, almost 50 million Americans (25% of adults) are believed to have metabolic syndrome. While only about 5% of teens have it, this percentage still represents over a million teenagers. The older you get, the more likely you are to develop metabolic syndrome, so almost half of those over 60 year of age meet the criteria. Seventy-five percent of those with metabolic syndrome are overweight.

Many people with metabolic syndrome also have elevated LDL (the "bad") cholesterol levels. Some people with metabolic syndrome have fatty liver and are therefore likely to have abnormal liver function tests. Others may have a skin disorder called acanthosis nigricans (which looks like a darker area of skin around the neck or in the armpits), which may be indicative of abnormal blood sugar levels. Women with the syndrome may have polycystic ovarian syndrome, which results in abnormal menstrual periods and infertility.

Each of these abnormalities on its own may not indicate a major health problem, but when they occur concurrently, they are an indication of risk of heart disease and diabetes. If you have any of these risk factors, ask your doctor to screen you for metabolic syndrome.

The Low-Carb Theory

Insulin has a number of important roles in the body, the most obvious of which is to help transport sugar from the blood into the cells. Insulin resistance occurs when the body needs more insulin than normal to do its job. Insulin also turns on fat storage inside the cell and turns off the process of burning fat for fuel. For this reason, it is difficult to lose weight when insulin levels are high.

Because insulin secretion is stimulated by eating sugar and carbohydrates, low-carbohydrate diets have become extremely popular. The theory is that if you avoid eating carbohydrates, you reduce your secretion of insulin and promote fat loss. While this theory is correct, the long-term health effects of low-carbohydrate diets are unknown. The other way to control insulin secretion is by eating more whole grains and avoiding refined carbohydrates (white bread, cakes, cookies, donuts, and anything made with sugar, corn syrup, or high-fructose corn syrup). This is a low-glycemic way to eat. Eating carbohydrates in the form of whole grains has repeatedly been shown to be associated with better health outcomes (unlike the low carbohydrate diets).

Whole grains are digested more slowly, releasing their sugar into the blood stream in a controlled fashion that allows the body to assimilate it without secreting large amounts of insulin. Nicola McKeown and colleagues analyzed data from the Framingham Offspring Cohort, which was published in both 2002 and 2004. They demonstrated that cereal fiber from whole grains was associated with protection against metabolic syndrome and that insulin sensitivity was negatively influenced by refined carbohydrate intake. This same group also observed that this relationship between whole-grain intake and fasting insulin was most significant among the study's overweight participants.

Bottom Line: Dietary Advice

Glucose intolerance: When you eat carbohydrates, your blood sugar goes up higher than normal and stays high longer than normal. The Insulin Resistance Atherosclerosis study showed that foods high in fiber, added to a low saturated fat diet, improve insulin sensitivity (thus reversing glucose intolerance).

Abdominal obesity: Studies have shown that fat stored around the belly is the most significant factor contributing to insulin resistance. This abdominal obesity is also the first fat lost when you go on a weight loss program. Incorporating whole grains, eating reasonable portion sizes, as well as exercising regularly, promote the loss of abdominal fat.

High blood pressure: If you have high blood pressure, the DASH diet (Dietary Approaches to Stop Hypertension) is the best way to lower your blood pressure. It is an important addition even if you need medication. DASH includes low-fat dairy and lots of fruits and vegetables, in addition to whole grains. In fact, in one study adding just two servings a day of soluble-fiber rich oats to the diet allowed 75% of people taking medication for their blood pressure to reduce their dose of medicine.

Abnormal lipid levels: Eating too many refined carbohydrates has also been linked to high triglyceride and low HDL cholesterol levels. Simple sugars increase your intake of whole grains and fiber-rich vegetables, and exercise regularly. If you smoke, do your best to stop. Cutting out cigarettes will also help to raise HDL levels. If your triglyceride levels are high (greater than 150 mg/dl), eliminate your alcohol intake.

Cancer

Cancer is a group of diseases characterized by the uncontrolled growth and spread of abnormal cells. Cancer is the second leading cause of death in the United States after heart disease. There are many different types of cancers, and the disease can affect organs (such as the colon, breast, or prostate) as well as tissues (such as the blood or bone). The most common types of cancer in the United States are skin, lung, breast, prostate, and colorectal.

Scientific evidence suggests that about one-third of cancer deaths in the United States each year are related to problems associated with poor nutrition, physical inactivity, and obesity. About 90,000 Americans die each year of cancers influenced primarily by obesity and excess weight, according to a recent study by the American Cancer Society. Obese people not only have a higher risk of developing cancer, but they also have a greater risk of dying from cancer. The American Cancer Society Cancer Prevention study of 900,000 U.S. adults showed that the death rates from all types of cancers combined were 52 percent higher in men and 62 percent higher in women who were obese compared to men and women who were at a normal weight. In this study the types of cancers more frequently linked with excess weight in women were breast, uterine, cervical, and ovarian. For men, the cancers frequently linked with excess weight were prostate, stomach, and colorectal.

In addition to excess weight, researchers have been working hard to uncover the links between diet and various forms of cancer and to identify the specific mechanisms that explain those relationships. Unfortunately, cancer is an extremely complicated process that develops over many years, and scientists working in this field have not been able to clearly determine its causes. Early studies identified clear links between environmental factors and cancer risk. For example, when people from Japan, where breast cancer rates are low, move to Hawaii, where cancer rates are much higher, their risk increases to that of native Hawaiians. This was initially presumed to be due to the increased amount of fat in the Hawaiian diet, but further efforts to confirm a link between dietary fat and breast cancer have not been successful.

The Miracle Workers: Whole Grains and Cancer Prevention

While scientific studies describing the benefits of whole grains for heart disease and diabetes are fairly clear and unambiguous, this is not the case for the relationship between whole grains and cancer risk. One problem is the fact that much of the research looks only at dietary fiber, which comes not only from grains but also from fruits and vegetables. These different food groups all make very important contributions to a healthy diet, so trying to determine which group (or what component) has what effect, has been difficult. In addition, fiber was initially seen as an inert substance that could not be digested by humans and therefore remained in the intestine. Now we know that there are compounds within the dietary fiber fraction of foods that are absorbed and metabolized by the body. In addition, the fiber that we don't metabolize is broken down by bacteria in the gut, yielding other chemicals (like short-chain fatty acids). These compounds have been shown to have effects both inside the intestine and on the cells that line the gut. Thus the relationship of fiber and cancers in different tissues is complex and still being discovered.

Fiber and Cancer

While the overall data linking dietary fiber and gastrointestinal cancers (colon, stomach, etc.) looks very promising, more recent research attempting to investigate the mechanisms responsible for fiber's protective effects has failed to confirm these early relationships. For example, when examining data from all over the world, there is a clear relationship between the weight of stool people produce and their risk of colon cancer. Since the fiber in grains increases fecal bulk, it reduces transit time (makes you go to the bathroom sooner) and thus is expected to reduce the exposure of intestinal cells to potential cancer-causing chemicals found in our diet. This is one possible way that fiber could be expected to reduce cancer risk.

Numerous studies have confirmed a link between the intake of whole grains and the risk of specific types of cancer. In fact, two meta-analysis studies have been completed that combine the findings of many other results and both concluded that increased fiber intake could lower the risk of colon or rectum cancer, pancreatic cancer, and stomach cancer by 20–40%. A large study in Europe confirmed the reduction in various forms of cancer in those who ate more whole grains. The Iowa Health Study in the United States in 2001 confirmed that whole-grain intake provided some level of protection from cancers that develop anywhere along the GI tract (from the mouth to the rectum). However, a number of studies designed to see if adding fiber to the diet would reduce the rate at which polyps develop in the colon (since most colon cancers develop from polyps) failed to show any decrease in polyp formation at the fiber doses that the previous epidemiologic studies would have predicted should have been protective.

While the situation with colon cancer is unclear, there are other forms of cancer that whole grains can help to protect against. Cancer of the uterus and ovaries (while much less common) are less likely to occur in women who eat whole grains on a daily basis. The Iowa Health Study documented almost 40% fewer endometrial (uterine) cancers in women who ate one to two servings of whole grains per day, compared to those who didn't.

While potential mechanisms for the protective effects of whole grains have been theorized, experiments continue in an effort to discover exactly how grains exert their protective effects and how powerful these effects are. For example, grains are a good source of lignan, which acts as a phytoestrogen (a plant-derived cousin of the human sex hormone). These compounds are believed to protect hormone-sensitive tissues (breast and uterus) by binding to the estrogen receptors and blocking the binding of natural estrogen (in this theory, too much natural estrogen is part of the cause of cancer). In support of this theory, the women in the Iowa Health Study who took hormone replacement therapy had no protection from endometrial cancer conferred by the whole grains in their diet.

Bottom Line: Dietary Advice

It remains to be determined whether it is the fiber in whole grains that is protective, the indigestible carbohydrates that are broken down by gut bacteria into short-chain fatty acids (these fatty acids reduce the conversion of bile acids into tumor-promoting forms), or the antioxidant properties that protect the cells that line the intestine. It is important to determine these mechanisms, because each grain has different components that will determine the specific health benefits. For instance, a study published by S. van Rensburg in 1981 comparing rates of cancer from different parts of the world, researchers found that in places where sorghum or millet was eaten, esophageal cancer rates were lower than in places where wheat or corn were more popular. They provided convincing evidence that the risk of esophageal cancer was related to nutrient deficiencies that were prevented in those consuming millet or sorghum.

Gastrointestinal Disease

The gastrointestinal (GI) tract is essentially a long tube. In total, it is about 24 feet (7¼ m) long and composed of a series of distinct sections starting from the mouth, and traveling through the esophagus, stomach, small and large intestine, rectum, and anus. Medically, the organs that contribute to GI function (particularly the pancreas, liver, and gall bladder) are also considered to be part of the GI tract. The GI organs are important to nutrition because they are where food is broken down to nutrients and where these nutrients are processed to be transported throughout the body for energy, growth, and repair. The GI tract is exposed directly to toxins in food and is responsible for eliminating much of the body's waste products.

The Role of Fiber in the GI Tract

Health professionals did not recognize the health impact of processing grains to remove their fiber (for example white rice from brown rice). However, scientists have now determined that fiber plays a vital role in the health of the GI tract, and that many components of fiber are broken down and some are actually absorbed, affecting both the gut and the body. While many of the health effects of whole grains can be attributed to their fiber content, researchers are increasingly recognizing that there is a synergy created by ingesting whole foods (the whole really is greater than the sum of the parts). In fact, recent studies suggested that there are active properties in whole grains that we have yet to identify.

Soluble vs. Insoluble Fibers

Some of the health benefits of specific whole grains depend upon the predominent fiber present in the grain. Grains that are good sources of soluble fiber (such as oats and barley) bind water in the upper GI tract (stomach and small intestine) and create a gel-like mixture. This gel slows the rate of gastric emptying, helping you to eat less because your stomach starts to feel full sooner. It also tends to slow down the absorption of sugar into the body, making these grains especially important for those with glucose intolerance and diabetes.

In the lower GI tract (large intestine and colon), this gel also blocks the absorption of bile acids, which in turn helps to lower cholesterol levels. This gel also binds fatty acids released during the digestion of fat in the diet and blocks their absorption, thus reducing some of the calories available for metabolism.

Grains high in insoluble fiber (such as whole wheat and rye) create bulk in the intestinal tract, making food move along faster through the gut. They have more of their impact at the lower end of the GI tract (particularly in the large intestine). By reducing the time available for digestive enzymes to break down large molecules, insoluble fiber reduces the calories available to be absorbed and causes more of the food that you eat to be delivered to the bacteria in your colon. It also causes a change in the type of bacteria present in the colon. This healthier bacteria produces less cancer-promoting compounds, which may explain the reduced risk of colon cancer associated with a high-fiber diet. The downside of this type of fiber is that it tends to promote gas production, which, while it has no negative health effects, may make you feel temporarily uncomfortable.

Colon Cancer and Fiber Intake

Denis Burkitt's original observations, made while he was a colonial health officer in Africa during the 1970s, documented that Africans who are on a high-fiber diet rarely if ever suffered from hemorrhoids, diverticulosis, or colon cancer. While the whites from Europe who lived in Africa, and those Africans who lived in cities and had adopted a more Westernized eating pattern, suffered from these disorders much more commonly. Over the past 35 years, numerous studies have confirmed the fact that dietary fiber seems to play a protective role in GI cancers (see cancer section, page 38).

Diverticulosis

Diverticulosis is the presence of small pouches, known as diverticuli, in the wall of the colon, which occur when parts of the intestine bulge outward through weak areas. The increase in pressure in the colon is commonly caused by constipation due to lack of fiber in the diet. From time to time one or more of these pouches become inflamed. Diverticulosis is common in the United States, England, and Australia where intake of fiber tends to be low. As people age, diverticulosis becomes increasingly common (more than half of 60-year-olds and nearly 100 percent of people over 80 in the United States have the disorder). The insoluble fiber in whole grains helps keep stools soft and easy to pass and prevents constipation.

Since there are very few symptoms associated with diverticulosis, at least 75 percent of the people who have this intestinal disorder are unaware of it. When symptoms are present, they may include mild abdominal cramps, bloating, or intermittent diarrhea or constipation. When the diverticuli become inflamed (a condition known as diverticulitis), people may develop tenderness in the lower abdomen, fever, nausea, vomiting, chills, cramping, and constipation.

Constipation

Constipation is defined as the infrequent (less than three times per week) and difficult passage of stools that are small and hard, which may result in straining to have bowel movements. According to the National Institute of Diabetes, Digestive, and Kidney Diseases, constipation is the most common gastrointestinal complaint in the United States, and accounting for about two million doctor visits each year. Because dietary fiber in food traps water and adds bulk to the stool, making it easier to move through the colon, constipation is usually the result of a diet containing inadequate fiber. A diet high in fiber from vegetables, fruits, and whole grains, is usually very effective at relieving the symptoms of constipation. Increasing exercise and drinking plenty of fluids is also part of the prescription.

Hemorrhoids

While not a serious medical condition, hemorrhoids are very common and cause a great deal of worry and annoyance to those who have them. To date there is no strong evidence that hemorrhoids can be prevented with a high-fiber diet, but it is certain that if you do have hemorrhoids, the presence of fiber in your diet will make your stool softer and easier to pass, thus making your hemorrhoids less likely to become inflamed and bleed.

Irritable Bowel Syndrome

An estimated 10–20% of Americans suffer from Irritable Bowel Syndrome (IBS); IBS is the ultimate diagnosis of up to 50% of patients referred to gastroenterologists. IBS causes symptoms of abdominal pain, with periods of constipation or diarrhea. Fiber may alleviate the constipation but otherwise does not seem to benefit those with IBS.

Gallstones

Gallstones are formed from bile, a cholesterol-rich liquid made by the liver and stored in the gallbladder that aids the digestive process. When the bile in the gallbladder has an excess concentration of cholesterol and becomes thickened into sludge, small and then larger stones can eventually form. Gallstones are more common in people over 40, and those who are overweight and eat a high-fat diet. Populations that eat less fat and more fiber tend to have lower risks of gallstones, as do those who weigh less. Thus whole grains may play a role both in helping with weight control and also by binding bile acids and leading to cholesterol excretion.

Celiac Disease: Not All Grains are Good for All People

Whole grains are especially healthful foods but, there are some people who cannot tolerate certain grains. People with celiac disease, a malabsorptive disorder also called *non-tropical sprue, or gluten intolerance,* have an intestinal allergy to gluten (one of the proteins afound in some grains). It is a genetic disease, meaning that it runs in families and occurs in both children and adults, affecting between 1 in 132 to 1 in 250 Americans. Wheat, rye, and barley are the most common offenders, with oats being somewhat controversial. Exposure to the gluten protein causes an inflammatory reaction in the cells lining the intestines of sensitive individuals. This leads to reduced absorption of calories from food and may be experienced as abdominal pain, gas, bloating, cramping, and diarrhea. This classical presentation of celiac disease may present itself within months of the introduction of wheat into a baby's diet and can cause growth failure, abdominal pain, and diarrhea. Others may develop gluten sensitivity later in life and begin to experience abdominal complaints (recurrent abdominal pain, nausea, vomiting, bloating, and constipation) around the age of five.

Silent Celiac Disease

While the clinical syndrome of celiac disease was initially believed to be restricted to those who had diarrhea with foul-smelling stools and weight loss, more recently "silent" forms of celiac disease have been described. People with "silent" celiac disease may have no symptoms at all for many years. Some complaints may be consistent with irritable bowel syndrome (abdominal pain, alternating constipation and diarrhea) or no intestinal symptoms but instead have lethargy (feeling tired all of the time) or develop anemia. If the untreated disease progresses, additional symptoms due to nutritional deficiency may appear.

Celiac disease has also been diagnosed in girls who are late starting their menstrual cycles or whose cycles are irregular, and some women with fertility have been cured by following a gluten-free diet. Unfortunately, 90% of the reported cases have been undiagnosed or misdiagnosed for 10 or more years.

Getting Tested

If you suspect that you have a problem digesting certain grains, or if you have symptoms that your doctor cannot explain, ask your doctor for an anti-gliadin antibody blood test. Since this is a genetic problem, family members of those who have been diagnosed should also be tested, even if there are no symptoms present. Gluten-free diets improve the symptoms, heal existing damage, and prevent further intestinal damage. Improvement begins within days of starting the diet, and the small intestine is usually healed and begins working properly in three to six months. For older adults, recovery may take up to two years. This gluten-free diet should be continued for life.

While difficult to recognize (because we may not think immediately about celiac disease when experiencing some of these symptoms, or the disease may be silent), the problems are reversible with the adoption of a gluten-free diet. The good news is that there are still many delicious whole grains that can be eaten even by those on a gluten-free diet as shown below. Each grain we highlight tells you

Whole Grains With and Without Gluten

Grains to Enjoy: Gluten-Free
Amaranth, Buckwheat, Corn, Millet, Quinoa, Rice, Sorghum, Teff

Grains To Avoid: Contains Gluten
Barley, Farro, Kamut, Oats, Rye, Spelt, Triticale, Wheat

whether or not it is safe for those with celiac disease and in the resource section we have included a list of websites and gluten-free product information on page 211.

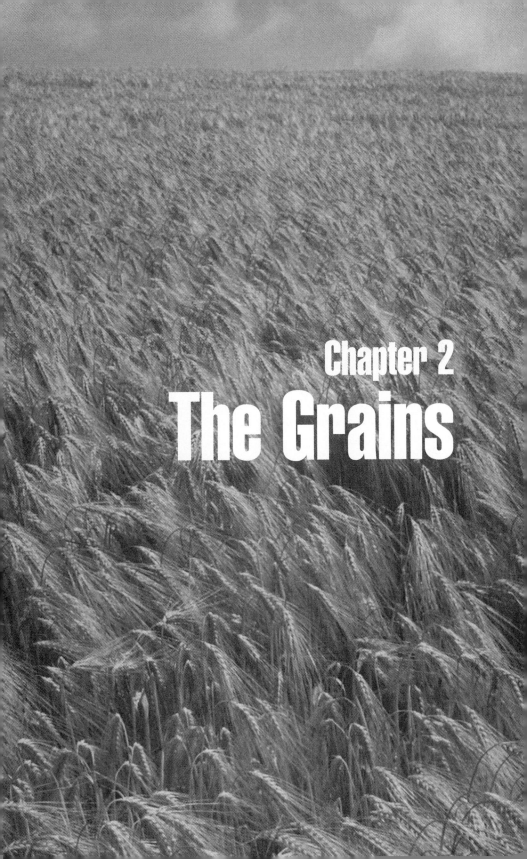

Chapter 2
The Grains

STORING WHOLE GRAINS

- Most whole grains, if kept uncooked in an airtight container in the refrigerator, can last for up to six months.
- Some whole grains can be stored in an airtight container in a cool, dry place. For instance, at room temperature, barley will remain fresh for six to nine months. If refrigerated, it will stay fresh for up to one year.
- If you live in a hot, humid climate, it is recommended to store all whole-grain products in the refrigerator or freezer.
- Buckwheat flour should be stored in the refrigerator and will keep fresh for several months. Millet flour, on the other hand, turns rancid quickly so it is recommended to grind it right before use, rather than storing it as flour.
- It is best not to let corn sit around for too long after buying it because it tends to lose its flavor quickly—plan on cooking and serving it as soon as possible. Refrigerate the corn in plastic bags and don't remove the husks until right before cooking. Freezing ears of corn for long periods of time is possible if you blanch them for 8 minutes, place them in sturdy freezer bags, and freeze for up to one year.
- To store popcorn properly, keep the kernels out of direct sunlight, as they can lose the moisture that allows them to pop so well. Airtight plastic or glass would do well for storage, especially if you place them in a cool, dry place. Refrigerating the popcorn is not your best bet, as that may dry out the delicate kernels.
- Storing uncooked brown rice in an airtight container in the refrigerator or freezer will keep it fresh for six months. After cooking, store leftover rice or teff in an airtight container in the refrigerator to keep it fresh for 3 to 5 days.

Amaranth is a grain with a gory past: the ancient Aztecs believed that amaranth seeds bore supernatural powers and represented human sacrifice. Aztec women mixed amaranth seeds with honey and human blood to shape idols that were eaten as part of religious ceremonies. When the Conquistadors confronted the Aztec civilization in the early 16th century, they were horrified by the practice of consuming blood and sacrificing humans. Believing they could stop these practices by outlawing amaranth, the Spanish quickly prohibited the cultivation of the grain. (This political decision is believed to have contributed to the ultimate demise of the Aztec culture.) Fortunately, the grain thrived in the region without human care, and grew wild for centuries.

Many years later amaranth experienced a renaissance in South America, and it is now an integral part of many cultures' ceremonies and daily diets. In Mexico, amaranth seeds are popped and served as a sweetened dessert. In Peru, women adorn themselves with amaranth flowers and bundles during their annual carnival. In other countries across the globe, amaranth seeds are eaten and the flowers are celebrated for their striking beauty.

In the 1970s, amaranth made its way to America, and today a few thousand acres are farmed each year in the Midwest. The plant is also cultivated throughout South America and South Asia.

Description

Not a true grain, amaranth is actually a hardy, bushy, flowering plant that can grow as tall as seven feet and is able to withstand both drought and extreme heat. The flowers of the amaranth plant are red or magenta in color and contain tiny edible seeds. Each plant produces 40,000 to 60,000 of these seeds, which are only $1/32$ of an inch in diameter. These seeds can be eaten as a cereal, milled into flour, sprouted, toasted, or popped like popcorn. One easy way to try amaranth is to add the grain to soups and stews as a healthful thickening agent.

Cooking Amaranth

To prepare amaranth, boil 3 cups of water for every 1 cup of amaranth. Boil for 18 to 20 minutes, until the seeds feel tender and slightly sticky.

Cooking Ideas:

- You can use amaranth flour to bake a variety of products. Because the flour is gluten-free, it must be mixed with a gluten-rich flour, such as whole wheat flour, in order to bake breads.
- Sprout amaranth seeds and use them in sandwiches and salads.
- Instead of boiling amaranth in water, use low-salt vegetable or chicken stock, or 100% apple juice for a unique, rich flavor.
- To make a hot breakfast cereal, boil amaranth in water and add sweetener such as honey, dried fruit, or maple syrup.

Nutritional Content

Amaranth seeds contain carbohydrates, protein, B vitamins, folate, phosphorus, calcium, magnesium, potassium, and iron. The fiber content of amaranth is three times higher than wheat.

Examples of Amaranth Products

Type of Amaranth Food	Serving Size	Total Calories	Dietary Fiber (g)
Amaranth Grain (uncooked)	¼ cup	170	3
Amaranth Flour	½ cup	220	4
Amaranth Flakes	1 cup	134	3.6
Amaranth Grits	¾ cup	170	5

Health Benefits

Amaranth contains tocotrienols (a form of vitamin E), which have been shown to lower blood cholesterol levels. Additionally, amaranth consists of 6-10% heart-healthy polyunsaturated oil, which is found mostly within the germ. The oil is high in linoleic acid which is thought to promote the body's anti-inflammatory process and prevent blood clotting. The grain is also gluten-free and appropriate for anyone with celiac disease or gluten intolerance.

Barley

Barley, one of the oldest grains in history, has played a very interesting role in many cultures, serving as food for humans and animals, a staple to make beer, and even as currency in Babylonian times. Originally from Ethiopia and Southeast Asia, barley has been used in recipes dating as far back as 2800 BC. Even the Bible refers to barley in breads made by the Hebrews, Romans, and Greeks. In addition, the Chinese have been cooking with barley for momre than 4,000 years. During the 16th century, barley was brought to South America by the Spanish and to the United States by English and Dutch settlers. Most likely, barley made its way to America because of its ability to germinate and produce malt, a key ingredient for the production of beer. Barely is harvested in the spring and is available year-round. The largest producers of barley are Canada, the United States, Russia, Germany, France, and Spain.

Description

Barely is available in a number of forms, including pearled, hulled, and flaked, which are described below. The grain consists of two outer husks, called the spikelet, which surround the cells of the endosperm. When barley is milled, the outer husks are removed, leaving the endosperm and making the grain edible. The final product is called pearled barley, a fiber-rich, nutrient-dense whole grain. Although all variations require some processing, barley maintains 50% of its original fiber content even after the bran is removed.

Hulled barley: With only its outer coating removed, hulled barley has the highest nutritional content of any barley product. The bran, which remains untouched, contains the majority of barley's fiber, vitamins, and minerals. Hulled barley is more difficult to obtain than other barley products and is most likely found in health food or specialty stores.

Pearled barley: The most readily available form of barley, pearled barley has the bran layer scrubbed off along with the outer hull, while the germ and the endosperm are left intact. "Lightly pearled" barley is a variety in which the bran coating is still present, producing a light brown color. Pearled barley is used in soups and dry baby cereal, and is a suprisingly delicious ingredient in salads and side dishes.

Heavily pearled barley: This processed barley resembles white rice in its appearance. Variations include small, fine, or baby pearled barley, which is used to make canned soups. Unlike other grains, barley contains fiber throughout its kernel, not just in the bran. Therefore, even in this highly processed form, barley contains some fiber.

Hull-less barley: This form of barley produces a hull that is loosely adhered to the kernel. This loose outer coating falls off of the kernel during harvesting, so minimal pearling is required. As more companies begin to produce whole grains, hull-less barley may become more available.

Cracked barley or barley flakes: These are flattened and sliced barley kernels that look similar to rolled oats and may be used for cereals.

Barley flour: Usually made from grinding pearled or hulled barley, this flour can be blended with whole wheat when baking. Because of its low gluten content, barley flour is ideal for people allergic to gluten.

Barley maintains **50%** of its **original fiber content** even after the bran is removed.

Cooking Barley

When preparing any type of barley, add 1 part barley to $3^1/_2$ parts boiling water. For added flavor, low-sodium chicken broth can also be substituted for water. Once the liquid is boiling, reduce heat, cover, and simmer for about one hour for pearled barley or 90 minutes for hulled barley. Make extra to keep in the refrigerator.

Cooking Ideas: With it sweet, nutty flavor, barley is a tasty addition to everything from soups to salads, breads to cereals.

- Cracked barley or barley flakes can be used for hot cereal or incorporated into baked goods, as described in our recipes.
- Barley flour, combined with wheat flour, is delicious in bread or muffin recipes.
- We have also developed traditional recipes using barley, such as soups and stews, and several interesting side dishes and salads.

Nutritional Content

Barley contains carbohydrates and protein, soluble and insoluble fiber, and is a rich source of thiamin, niacin, selenium, iron, zinc, phosphorus, copper, and manganese. One cup of cooked barley contains about 50% of the daily requirements for selenium, an important trace mineral required for normal thyroid hormone metabolism, antioxidant defense systems, and immune function. Adequate selenium intake has also been shown to reduce the risk of developing cancer, which is discussed further in the health benefits section.

Each type of barley varies in its nutritional content and recommended use, with hulled barley having the highest fiber content and heavily pearled having the least. While pearled barley is processed, it still contains a significant amount of fiber. When teamed with vegetables in side dishes and salads, barley contributes to fiber-packed, nutritious grain dishes.

Examples of Barley Products

Type of Barley Food	Serving Size	Total Calories	Dietary Fiber (g)
Hulled barley (cooked)	1 cup	270	14
Pearled barley (cooked)	1 cup	193	6
Barley and mushroom soup	1¼ cup	230	6
Baby food, barley cereal with whole milk	1 oz (25 g)	31	0
Barley flour	1 cup	511	15

Health Benefits

The majority of the studies looking at the health benefits of barley have been conducted in conjunction with other whole grains. The benefits related to barley are likely due to its high fiber content, both soluble and insoluble, as well as the antioxidant properties of selenium. Thus, eating barley can be expected to contribute to preventing both heart disease and cancer.

Buckwheat

Once used only as animal feed and fertilizer, buckwheat has now become a staple for bakers, beekeepers, and health-conscious cooks. Originally cultivated in Central Asia and China in the 10th century, buckwheat made its way to Europe via migrations of people from Siberia and Manchuria. Because of its versatility, buckwheat became a mainstay in the cuisines of Finland, Austria, northern Italy, France, Russia, and Eastern Europe. German and Dutch settlers brought buckwheat to the United States in the 17th century and planted expansive fields in the New York area. Beekeepers soon noticed that the fragrant nectar of the buckwheat blossom allowed bees to produce honey with an intense, delectable flavor.

Today, buckwheat noodles, referred to as soba noodles, are a popular alternative to traditional pasta. Buckwheat can also be used to make delicious, hearty pancakes, breads, muffins, crackers, tortillas, and even cookies. Buckwheat flour is easy to find in supermarkets and health food stores and can be mixed with wheat flour to give baked products a distinctive, nutty flavor.

Description

Despite its name, buckwheat is not actually related to wheat at all. Buckwheat is an herbaceous plant from the Polygonaceae family. Unlike other grains, it does not grow as a grass, but rather a low-lying, flowering plant.

Japanese buckwheat: Most of the buckwheat grown in the United States is Japanese buckwheat, which is milled and ground into flour for use in pancakes, breads, and muffins.

Raw groats: Buckwheat groats are light brown in color and have a mild, slightly bitter flavor. Raw groats are buckwheat kernels that are stripped of their outer, inedible hull and compressed into small pieces. To remove their bitter flavor, raw groats may be roasted in oil for several minutes until they achieve a deep, rust color.

Roasted groats: Also known as kasha, these are dark brown in color, with an intense, nutty flavor and aroma. They are usually toasted in oil and can be used to make blintzes, knishes, pilaf, and hot cereal.

Buckwheat grits: Eaten as a hot cereal, these finely ground buckwheat groats cook quickly when boiled. Other names for buckwheat grits are *cream of buckwheat* and *buckwheat cereal.*

Cooking Buckwheat

Before cooking, rinse buckwheat briefly under cool, running water to remove any debris. If you are using raw groats, toast them lightly in oil until they reach a deep brown color. To cook, add 1 cup of buckwheat to 2 cups boiling water or low-sodium broth. Once the liquid returns to a boil, turn down the heat, cover, and simmer for 15 to 20 minutes. Buckwheat is a very porous grain and has the tendency to absorb all of the liquid in the pot. Check the buckwheat frequently, adding liquid if necessary to avoid burning the bottom of the pot.

Cooking Ideas:

- Boil buckwheat as suggested above, and combine with low-fat milk and honey for a tasty breakfast alternative to oatmeal.
- Use soba noodles instead of traditional pasta.
- Add leftover chicken or tofu to a serving of cooked buckwheat for a quick and hearty lunch.
- Include buckwheat in soup recipes for added texture and flavor.
- In any standard baking recipe, substitute $1/3$ to $1/2$ cup of buckwheat flour per cup of higher gluten flour (unbleached white flour or wheat flour) for more flavorful baked goods.
- Add $1/2$ cup of cooked buckwheat to your salads.

Nutritional Content

Buckwheat is an excellent source of carbohydrates, manganese, magnesium, thiamin, riboflavin, fiber, and protein. Because it is not actually a variety of wheat, people who are allergic to gluten may add buckwheat to their diet.

Examples of Buckwheat Products

Type of Buckwheat Food	Serving Size	Total Calories	Dietary Fiber (g)
Buckwheat pancakes, dry mix	1 oz (25 g)	96	2
Buckwheat flour, whole-groats	½ cup	200	6
Kasha (buckwheat groats) (cooked)	1 cup	155	5
Buckwheat rice cakes	1 cake	34	0
Soba noodles (cooked)	1 cup	113	0

Health Benefits

Diets rich in buckwheat are known to lower cholesterol and blood pressure. After studying the Yi people of China, a population that generally consumes 100 grams of buckwheat daily, scientists concluded that buck-

Diets **rich in buckwheat** have been shown to **aid in the management** of diabetes.

wheat consumption lowers total blood cholesterol and LDL cholesterol (the bad cholesterol) levels while improving the ratio of HDL to LDL cholesterol.

Diets rich in buckwheat have also been shown to aid in the management of diabetes. Other studies show that bread made of buckwheat groats considerably lowers blood glucose and insulin response after consumption. In addition, the magnesium in buckwheat can contibute to lowering the risk of diabetes by as much as 24%. Magnesium is also known to relax blood vessels, lowering blood pressure and improving nutrient delivery to cells.

Corn

That fresh corn on the cob we love to enjoy at summer picnics and family barbecues has a lot of history behind it. Thought to have originated in Central America, it has served as a staple food to native civilizations in primitive times and continues to hold a central place in the diets of Native American cultures today. Because of their heavy reliance on corn for sustenance, the Mayan, Aztec, and Incan civilizations regarded corn as a sacred food and incorporated it into their mythology and rituals. Early explorers discovered corn growing all across America in solid, smooth, and striped varieties, as well as a bright array of colors such as blue, pink, yellow, and black. When Spanish and Portuguese explorers returned from the New World, they brought corn home with them, soon spreading corn around the world.

It is interesting to note that traditional Native American corn dishes were often mixed and served with lime, a calcium oxide mineral compound made by burning limestone. Because limestone occurs naturally in the United States, it was often derived from the process of burning wood into ash, which was then added into corn dishes. Native Americans had discovered that something in limestone improved health, and they were right. Niacin (vitamin B_3) is not easily absorbed from corn on its own, but lime helps to free this vitamin and thus the body is able to absorb and metabolize it. In fact, southerners soak their corn in lime water to make hominy grits.

Corn can be boiled whole and consumed as a tasty vegetable, or milled into cornmeal and incorporated into recipes. Today, the largest amounts of this important crop are grown in the United States, Russia, China, Mexico, and Brazil. In the United States, millions of bushels of corn are grown each year for domestic use as food, animal feed, and for commerical uses, such as the production of corn syrup. In addition, corn is the United States's primary agricultural export.

Description

Known scientifically as *Zea mays*, corn grows in "ears" that are dotted with rows of kernels and cushioned by silky fibers, or "corn silk." The rigid green husk around the ear provides excellent protection from the elements. The original corn of around 5000 BC is thought to have possessed few kernels. After thousands of years of domestication, the natives developed techniques for producing plump, kernel-filled ears.

Cornmeal: Cornmeal, or milled corn, can be used to make anything from pancakes to breads. Usually, corn undergoes a milling process in which the ears are cleaned, steamed, the husks removed, and the corn ground, leaving only the endosperm of the kernel as cornmeal. The cornmeal is then enriched to replace the nutrients lost during milling. It is therefore best to purchase stoneground cornmeal, which is coarsely ground in a way that allows the rich germ inside to remain intact. Cornmeal comes in yellow and white varieties depending on whether it's made from yellow or white corn. Yellow corn grits are also available in health food stores. For those with gluten allergies, cornmeal products provide wonderful alternatives to wheat as they are gluten-free.

Popcorn: Long before explorers landed on American shores, the Native Americans were popping corn in pottery crocks over sand and decorating themselves with popcorn necklaces and ceremonial headdresses. Some tribes believed that spirits lived in the popcorn kernels and became angry if someone tried to heat them up—when they could no longer contain their anger, they would break through the walls and pop out. In more recent times, popcorn has stood the test of time as a fun, healthy, and popular snack. It became common in the late 1800s and reached its heights during the Great Depression as a hearty and cheap snack even the poorest families could afford. Today, North Americans consume about 17 million quarts of popcorn each year!

Popcorn is an excellent snack that both kids and adults can enjoy, and best of all, it's fat-free, sugar-free, has no artificial additives, and few calories when air-popped. Popcorn won't spoil your appetite between meals and can be creatively incorporated into many fun recipes.

How exactly does popcorn pop? The starchy bran and germ surround the endosperm, which actually contains some water. When the kernel is heated, the water begins to expand and press on the bran surrounding it. When the bran can't take any more pressure, it explodes and the endosperm bursts, turning the kernel inside out. As the built-up steam flows out, we take out the freshly popped corn and smell that deliciously unmistakable popcorn aroma.

Polenta: Originating as a prime sustenance of Italian peasants in the countryside, polenta is popular in homes around the world as a simply prepared, tasty side dish. Before the introduction of corn into Europe in the 1700s, polenta was made from various other grains and legumes, seasoned with oils and spices, and boiled into a fine, consistent mush. With the arrival of milled corn in the form of cornmeal, it became a popular replacement for other grains when making polenta. Today, polenta is loved by many people because it is delicious and nutritious, either on its own or as an accompaniment to other dishes. Polenta is easy to make, or for convenience, you can buy ready-to-eat polenta at most markets.

Cooking Corn

Corn: Corn can be boiled or steamed quite easily without its husk or roasted in the husk. Just make sure not to overcook the ears, as they may become rigid and lose their flavor. If you choose to roast the ears in the husk, be sure to soak them first. One popular method is to open the husk carefully to remove the silk, season with olive oil, salt and pepper, and then fold back the husks and roast on low heat on a barbecue grill.

Polenta: Making polenta from scratch requires time and lots of stirring. Boil 2 quarts (2 liters) of water. As the pot continues to boil, pour in 1 pound (450 g) of coarsely ground cornmeal, and stir mixture. Keep stirring in the same direction for about 20 to 30 minutes. The longer you stir it, the better it will turn out. Once it is done, it has a puddinglike consistency. You can either serve it as is, or sprinkled with parmesan cheese, topped with sautéed vegetables, or served alongside chicken, fish, or lean meat.

Cooking Ideas:

- Add popcorn to your favorite trail mix recipes for extra fiber.
- To spice up your popcorn, add oregano, pepper, and garlic powder to the popping oil.
- Top hearty salads and hot soups with popcorn.
- To make corn on the cob even more tasty, season it with flax seed oil, olive oil, and any of your favorite spices.
- Add cooked corn to chowders, soup, and stews.
- Add cooked corn to salads and stir-fry dishes.

Nutritional Content

Corn is considered a starchy vegetable because of its high carbohydrate content. It is also abundent in thiamin, folate, dietary fiber, vitamin C, phosphorus, and manganese. Corn is low in fat, is a good source of soluble and insoluble fiber, and is appropriate in the diets of anyone allergic to gluten.

Examples of Corn Products

Type of Corn Food	Serving Size	Total Calories	Dietary Fiber (g)
Corn, yellow	½ cup	66	2
Corn flour, whole-grain, white	1 cup	422	11
Corn flakes, cereal	1 cup	101	1
Polenta (cooked)	¼ cup	130	2
Popcorn (air-popped)	3 cups	93	3

Growing wildly throughout the Fertile Crescent (south of Jerusalem, northward along the Mediterranean coast to Syria, eastward through Iraq, and south to the Persian Gulf), farro is one of the oldest grains on earth. Evidence of wild farro dates back to the Paleolithic era of 17,000 BC. Cultivation of farro, along with wheat and barley, began about 10,000 years ago in the Near and Far East, Europe, and North Africa. In the ancient Roman Empire, farro was the food of choice for armies because it was easy to produce and rich in nutrients. Development of farro eventually slowed throughout the Middle Ages as farmers began to favor wheat, barley, and other newly cultivated grains. By 1900, farro was only cultivated in parts of Russia, Italy, Ethiopia, and India. Today, farro remains a staple crop of Ethiopia and is used as a gourmet ingredient in Italian kitchens. Fortunately for Americans, health food stores are beginning to stock farro in bulk, and a number of upscale restaurants incorporate farro into their dishes.

Description

Deriving its name from the Italian word *farina*, meaning flour, farro is an ancient relative of both spelt and durum wheat. Farro, and its "cousins" emmer and einkorn, are known as "hulled wheats," meaning the berry or kernel retains its hull during harvest and must be dehulled prior to further processing. The edible portion of the grain grows within the hull, which protects it from environmental damage and contamination from pesticides.

Cooking Farro

Rinse farro in cool water to remove any dust and debris from the grains, then soak it for at least eight hours before cooking. If desired, farro can soak for up to two days in the refrigerator prior to cooking. Once ready to cook, boil farro in the water used for soaking for approximately two hours. Remove from heat and allow the grains to sit for several minutes so they can fully absorb any remaining liquid. Well-prepared farro has a texture that is both chewy and firm. To cut cooking time in half, prepare farro in a pressure-cooker.

Cooking Ideas:
- Farro semolina, a coarsely ground flour, is ideal for making home-made pasta.
- Add cooked farro to salads and hearty soups for an exciting flavor.
- Serve farro as a side dish instead of rice or pasta.
- For extra flavor, boil farro in low-salt vegetable or chicken stock.

Nutritional Content

Farro is an exceptional source of fiber, magnesium, and vitamins A, B, C, and E. Farro has low gluten content, which allows many people who are sensitive to gluten to enjoy the grain without allergic symptoms. If you are allergic to gluten, talk to a physician or nutritionist knowledgeable in this area before making any changes in your diet.

Health Benefits

Farro has yet to be the focus of any major clinical studies, but its rich nutrients shows that it is an excellent choice for health and nutrition.

Kamut

Legend has it that kamut entered the United States after a U.S. airman discovered the grains hidden within an ancient Egyptian stone box. Bringing back only a handful of kernels, the airman gave them to a friend to farm. The kamut crop was an amusing sight: the plants looked exactly like common wheat, only enormous! The farmer called his plant "King Tut's Wheat" and sold it as a novelty item at state fairs.

Whether the tale is fact or simply lore, it is true that kamut is an ancient relative to common wheat, originating in the Fertile Crescent. In fact, kamut earned its name from the ancient Egyptian word for "wheat," which also means, "soul of the earth."

One of kamut's most exceptional qualities is its ability to thrive without the use of fertilizers and pesticides. Growing particularly well under the strict conditions set by organic farmers, kamut is becoming more popular as the demand for organic farming increases worldwide.

Description

Although it looks similar to durum wheat, kamut contains 20–40% more protein, fats, vitamins, and minerals. Naturally sweet and buttery in flavor, kamut is delicious in cereals, baked goods, and breads. Kamut's firm kernels also lend themselves to delicious pilafs and pastas.

Cooking Kamut

To cook kamut, boil 1 cup of the grain in 3 cups of water, adding a dash of salt. The grain will cook in about two hours.

Cooking Ideas:

- Kamut is tasty both hot and cold, especially in side dishes or salads.
- Look for kamut pastas and breads, both of which are praised for their exceptionally sweet flavor.
- Combine kamut with rice or whole grains for added texture.
- Make a hot breakfast cereal from kamut, milk, vanilla, and raisins.

Nutritional Content

Kamut is an excellent source of protein, essential fatty acids, vitamins, and minerals. Kamut is a good source of the selenium, magnesium, zinc, and vitamin E. This grain contains gluten and should be not be eaten by anyone with a gluten sensitivity or wheat allergy.

Examples of Kamut Products			
Type of Kamut Food	Serving Size	Total Calories	Dietary Fiber (g)
Kamut flour	¼ cup	94	3
Puffed kamut cereal	1 cup	50	2
Kamut flakes	1 cup	120	2
Kamut pizza	1 slice	330	9

Health Benefits

As a newly discovered grain, kamut has not yet been the focus of many scientific studies. However, with its array of vitamins, minerals, amino acids, and antioxidants, kamut surely offers many of the same health benefits as whole wheat.

Millet

Millet is one of the oldest and most nutritious grains in the world. Originating in the Ethiopian region of Africa in prehistoric times, it was even discussed in the Bible as an ingredient in unleavened bread. Millet has long been an important food staple in both Africa and India, where it is still used to make the traditional African flatbread, injera, and the Indian flatbread, roti. During the Middle Ages, millet became popular in Eastern Europe, where it was used in the preparation of traditional dishes like porridge and kasha. Millet was introduced to the United States in the 18th century by settlers from Europe. Although it was used primarily as birdseed and livestock fodder, millet is now gaining momentum as a healthful grain for North Americans' everyday diet. Today, the main worldwide producers are India, China, and Nigeria. In the United States, most millet is grown in Colorado, North Dakota, and Nebraska.

Description

The term millet may refer to a variety of grains, most of which is used as birdseed and not consumed as food. The millet that you are most likely to see in your local grocery or health food store is generally classified as *Panicum miliaceuem* or *Setaria italica*. There are four major varieties of millet—Pearl, Foxtail, Finger, and Proso millet. Pearl millet is the largest of the four and mostly used for food products.

Millet looks like a tall grass that is similar to maize. The millet seeds are surrounded by a hard, indigestible hull, and so they have to be hulled in order to be used for human consumption. Because the germ remains intact, hulling does not affect the nutrient value of the grain. Millet seeds are small, round, and pearly looking. They come in a variety of colors: yellow, white, gray, or red. Millet is a versatile grain that can grow in many different regions. It grows well in climates with both high and low temperatures, needs little moisture, and has a short growing season.

Millet, like buckwheat, does not contain gluten and can be included in a gluten-free diet. It also does not form acid, making it quite easy to digest for those who have celiac disease.

Cooking Millet

You can use millet to make just about anything from cereals, casseroles, and breads to stews, pilafs, and stuffing. You can make it as a side dish by mixing it with vegetables or combining it with a variety of spices and other grains for flavorful salads.

Before cooking, wash the millet to remove dirt and sift through to remove any damaged grains. To cook, combine 1 cup millet with 3 cups of boiling water, and cook for about 30 minutes or until you see that the water has been absorbed by the grain. Remove from heat and leave covered for about 10 more minutes.

Millet flour: Ground from millet, millet flour produces light, delicate baked goods. If you wish to use it in yeast breads, use only up to 30% and make the rest gluten-containing flour so the bread will rise. If you want to add a crunch to your baked goods, you can even add in raw millet seeds before baking them.

Cooking Tips:
- If you pre-soak millet beforehand, cooking time can decrease by 5 to 10 minutes.
- If you prefer a fluffier texture, use less water, but if you'd like a dense texture, use more water.

- To improve millet's flavor, you may wish to roast it in a pan before cooking—stir for about 3 minutes on low heat or until you detect a nutty, burning aroma. Once you see a golden color appear, add boiling water.
- To vary the consistency and flavor, you may wish to experiment with cooking times and methods.

Nutritional Content

Its tasty, mildly sweet, nutlike quality makes millet ideal for a variety of recipes. Composed mostly of carbohydrates, it also has 15% protein, lots of fiber, and B vitamins such as niacin, thiamin, and riboflavin.

Examples of Millet Products

Type of Millet Food	Serving Size	Total Calories	Dietary Fiber (g)
Millet (cooked)	1 cup	207	2
Puffed millet	1 cup	74	1
Millet flour	¼ cup	110	4
Millet mashers	1 cup	150	5

Health Benefits

Millet is rich in phytochemicals like phytate, which are thought to reduce the risk of cancer, and phytic acid, which may lower cholesterol levels.

Oats

Although oats have become quite popular as a nutritious breakfast food, their origins were much more humble. Deriving from the wild red oat plant in Asia, oats are believed to have grown as uncultivated weeds in the presence of other crops. The domestication of oats occurred around 2500 BC, probably in northern Africa, the Near East, and the temperate areas of Russia. For the past 2,000 years, the grain has been cultivated throughout the world. Before gaining wide acceptance as a food staple, oats were often used as animal feed, bedding for livestock, or for medicinal purposes such as treating rashes and dry skin. For thousands of years, Europe was the center of commercial oat production, and oats figured prominently in the diets of people in Scotland, Great Britain, Germany, and Scandinavia. Their North American debut came in the early 17th century when Scottish settlers first planted oats along the coast of Massachusetts. Initially relying on oats as feed for poultry and livestock, North Americans eventually came to regard this grain as a nutritionally beneficial part of their own everyday diet.

Oats are typically harvested in the fall and available year round. Today, the grain is produced and consumed all over the world. Because oats are hardy and can withstand poor soil conditions unsuitable for other grains, they thrive in various regions. Currently, the major commercial producers of oats include Russia, Germany, Poland, Finland, and the United States.

Description

Oats (*Avena sativa*) undergo special processing after being harvested to provide consumers with a variety of products. Although all oats are hulled, this process does not strip away the bran and germ, allowing oats to retain their exclusive flavor, along with a multitude of nutrients and fiber.

Old-fashioned rolled oats: These are the most well-known form of oats and are widely available at the grocery store. Their flat shape results from being hulled, steamed, and then pressed with steel rollers. They puff up quickly when cooked (5 to 7 minutes) and are easy to chew and digest. They are the preferred type of oats for oatmeal, granola, and fruit cobblers.

Quick oats: These grains are just like old-fashioned oats, except they are sliced thinly before being rolled. This allows them to cook more rapidly (3 to 5 minutes). They are the preferred type of oats for making oatmeal cookies.

Instant oats: Loved by many for their convenience, these oats are made of groats that have been cut into tiny pieces, then precooked, dried, and rolled very thin. Flavored varieties generally include sugar, salt, and other ingredients. To make, just add hot water, stir, and enjoy.

Oat groats (whole oats): This variety involves the minimal processing, only removing the hull. Because groats can be difficult to chew, they require more cooking time, about 50 minutes, and more water. They are best for breakfast cereals, hearty breads, and flavorful salads.

Steel-cut oats (Irish oats): Chewier than rolled oats, these are often used for hot cereal in Ireland and Scotland. Steel-cut oats are actually oat groats chopped into small pieces. Also called "Irish oats" or "Scotch oats," they are used to make oatmeal porridge.

Oat flour: Used in pancakes, muffins, biscuits, and other baked products, this flour is made by grinding groats into a fine powder. You can produce your very own oat flour by grinding rolled oats in a blender. It is used as a thickening agent in broths, soups, and sauces and contains most of the nutrients found in whole oats.

Oat bran: Rich in fiber and other nutrients, this outer layer of the grain is found under the hull and is removed from the groats during further processing. Although oat bran can be found in rolled oats and steel-cut oats, it can also be purchased separately. Oat bran is very versatile and can be added to hot and cold cereals, as well as used in muffins, cakes, and breads. However, it is best to avoid commercial oat-bran muffins, as they often contain more than 500 calories and lots of fat.

Cooking Oats

Oats are usually found in your local supermarket either prepackaged or in bulk bins. Before purchasing, make sure the store has a good turnover to ensure freshness, that the oat bins are securely covered, and that the oats are free of debris and moisture. Smelling the oats is also a good way of determining whether they are fresh. They should not smell rancid. When buying oats, it is always wise to do so in small quantities because oats have a slightly higher fat content than other grains and may turn rancid more quickly. If you buy a prepared product like oatmeal, look at the ingredients to ensure that the product contains no salt, sugar, or artificial additives.

When cooking any kind of oat product, it is best to use twice as much water as oats—that is, 2 cups water to 1 cup oats. Add the oats to cold water and bring them to a boil. Because oat groats are thicker than other oats, they require 3 parts water to 1 part groats and should be cooked for a longer time (about 50 minutes). Remember, the longer the cooking time, the more nutritious the oats will be because it means that there is more fiber, especially the soluble type.

Cooking Ideas: Oats add great taste and texture to any meal, and best of all, they go a long way toward boosting your fiber intake. Enjoy these great oat ideas any time of day.

- Sprinkle your favorite cereal with oat bran.
- Add oat flour to your favorite baked goods.
- Use old-fashioned oats as a topping for fruit crisps and cobblers.
- Try ground oats as breading for fish or chicken.
- Make your own oat-based granola (see recipe on page 155).

Nutritional Content

Oats contain carbohydrate, protein, and fiber and are also a rich source of thiamin, selenium, phosphorus, and manganese. They contain smaller amounts of copper, folate, vitamin E, and zinc. Some quick-cooking oat packets are also enriched with vitamins and minerals, such as iron.

Examples of Oat Products

Type of Oat Food	Serving Size	Total Calories	Dietary Fiber (g)
Old-fashioned oats (cooked)	1 cup	147	4
Instant oatmeal (apple-spice flavored)	1 packet	169	3
Oatmeal cookies (2½-inch, 6¼ cm, diameter)	2 cookies	190	1
Oatmeal bread (reduced calorie)	1 slice	48	0
Oat waffles (round, 4-inch, 10 cm, diameter)	1 waffle	69	1
Oat bran bagel (4-inch, 10 cm, diameter)	½ bagel	114	1.5

Health Benefits

Eating oatmeal and other oat products on a daily basis is a great way to maintain a healthy weight or lose weight, lower cholesterol, boost heart health, and prevent or manage diabetes. Much of oatmeal's disease-fighting power comes from its rich amounts of fiber—nearly 55% soluble fiber and 45% insoluble fiber. In fact, the Food and Drug Administration has approved the health claim: *"Soluble fiber from oatmeal, as part of a low saturated fat, low cholesterol diet, may reduce the risk of heart disease."* Soluble fiber dissolves in water and turns into a viscous gel when digested, which moves very slowly through the intestinal tract. This may explain why eating oats has been shown to reduce the absorption of sugar, thereby benefiting people with diabetes. In fact, oats contain more soluble fiber than any other grain.

Oats have also been shown to reduce inflammation, especially in the skin. A number of skin lotions and bath products use oats to soften the skin and reduce itching.

Quinoa

Native to the mountains of South America, quinoa was the esteemed dietary staple of the ancient Incas. Championing it for its ability to grow in the poor, arid soil of the Andes, the Incas began cultivating this grain over 5,000 years ago. Quinoa was renowned for its ability to bring stamina and health to Inca warriors, earning the grain its titles, "the gold of the Incas" and "the mother seed." The grain was so vital that, when the Spanish Conquistadors invaded, they destroyed the sprawling fields of quinoa, knowing the population relied upon the grain for survival. Additionally, the conquistadors made it illegal for the Incas to grow quinoa, punishing the crime with death. Fortunately, the hearty grain thrived in the Andean soil and survived the Spanish invasion.

In North America, the benefits of quinoa remained virtually unknown until the 1980s. It was only then that farmers, upon learning of quinoa's extraordinary nutritional content and creamy, light flavor, began cultivating it in the Colorado Rockies. Ever since, quinoa has grown in popularity, and it is now widely imported from Bolivia, Ecuador, and Chile, while still being produced in the Colorado Rockies.

Description

Although quinoa is typically classified as a grain, it is, in fact, a vegetable seed. With the scientific name *Chenopodium quino*, the plant is distantly related to spinach, beets, and Swiss chard. The seeds of the plant are small, with a flattened oval shape. Colors range from yellow to red, purple to black. The most widely eaten variety of quinoa is a pale, nearly translucent yellow.

Quinoa grain: Known for its milky, light, and subtle flavor, quinoa is also thought to be one of the world's healthiest grains.

Quinoa pasta: A perfect choice for anyone looking for delicious, gluten-free pasta, quinoa pasta comes in a variety of shapes and flavors. Quinoa pastas are gaining popularity, increasingly becoming available in health food stores nationwide.

Quinoa flour: To bake with quinoa, substitute all-purpose flour with quinoa flour and reduce the measurements by half. If replacing whole-wheat flour, follow the recipe's recommended measurements. Because it has a higher fat content than traditional flour, quinoa produces moist and delicious baked goods.

Cooking Quinoa

Before cooking quinoa, rinse it thoroughly under cool water to remove the saponin, a soaplike layer that has a bitter flavor and can potentially irritate the digestive tract. After rinsing, combine 1 cup of quinoa with 2 cups of water and bring to a boil. Once the mixture boils, reduce the heat, cover, and simmer until the water is absorbed. One serving of quinoa normally cooks within 10 or 15 minutes. Before serving, allow the quinoa to steam for five minutes and then fluff with a fork.

Cooking Ideas:
- Add raisins, honey, walnuts, and a chopped apple to a serving of quinoa for a delicious breakfast.
- Instead of white rice, use quinoa to prepare tabbouleh, pilaf, stir-fry, and other favorite rice dishes.
- Make a delightful pudding with quinoa, milk, honey, and cinnamon.

- To make a delicious butternut squash with stuffing, mix toasted nuts, dried fruits, and a touch of brown sugar in a bowl with cooked quinoa and bake in a halved squash.
- Add black beans, corn, and spices to a cup of cooked quinoa for a tasty salad.

Nutritional Content

Quinoa is an excellent source of carbohydrates, as well as high-quality protein because it contains all of the essential amino acids, including lysine, methionine, and cystine. In addition, quinoa is low in fat, high in fiber, gluten-free, and is a good source of iron, magnesium, potassium, B vitamins, and calcium.

Examples of Quinoa Products

Type of Quinoa Food	Serving Size	Total Calories	Dietary Fiber (g)
Quinoa grain (cooked)	¼ cup	160	6.5
Quinoa flour	¼ cup	120	2
Quinoa pasta (cooked)	2 oz (50 g)	180	2.5
Quinoa tuna sandwich	1 sandwich	240	8

Health Benefits

Purported to be the most nutritious grain in the world, quinoa has the ability to improve health from head to toe. For anyone who suffers from migraines, incorporating quinoa into the diet is a wise decision. The magnesium found in quinoa relaxes blood vessels, reducing the frequency of migraine headaches. Quinoa has also been found to improve energy metabolism in brain and muscle cells, which may lead to fewer headaches. The high fiber content of quinoa has been shown to lower cholesterol and blood pressure, and reduce the risk of gallstone formation and heart disease. Introducing this "super food" into your diet is a smart and tasty choice.

Rice

For much of the world, rice is the essence of the daily diet. Cultivated more than 6,000 years ago in Asia, rice is both a cultural and nutritional staple across the world. An ancient Chinese religious ceremony centered upon the Emperor's sowing of the annual rice, marking the significance of rice in the ancient world. Buddhism carried rice throughout Asia, ensuring the nutritional, religious, and political importance of rice across the continent. After their invasion of India, the armies of Alexander the Great brought rice to Europe. By the 17th century, rice was cultivated in Africa, Asia, Europe, and North America.

Today, rice is so pervasive that, in many languages, the verb "to eat" is derived from the phrase "to eat rice." In many countries, rice symbolizes fertility and is thrown at weddings to wish fertility upon the bride and groom. With nearly 200 billion pounds produced each year, the popularity of rice is assured.

Unfortunately, much of the rice produced each year goes through a complicated machine-milling process to produce white rice. The husk, bran layer, and the germ of the rice kernel are removed, leaving behind only the endosperm, which makes up 75% of the rice kernel and consists of mostly starch. The discarded bran and germ layers contain the kernel's fiber, a small amount of fat, and protein, vitamins, and minerals.

In less industrialized countries, many farmers process their rice by hand in a method called "hand-pounding." Using a mortar and pestle, the farmers grind away the kernel's bran layer, leaving the majority of the germ intact. Hand-pounding preserves more of rice's nutrients than does machine-milling. The purest form of rice is whole-grain brown rice, in which only the inedible husk is removed.

Description

Brown rice (*Oryza Sativa*) and wild rice (*Zizania aquatica*) are actually two entirely separate species of grass. Although there are 20 known species of brown rice, the most widely cultivated species are the Asian and African varieties. Between the two species, more than 50,000 varieties of brown rice exist.

Despite its name, wild rice is not actually rice at all. A member of the grass family, wild rice flourishes without cultivation on the banks of the Great Lakes and other North American wetlands. Because the plant grows wild, 60% of the annual crop is lost, making wild rice a specialty food. Try wild red rice from Italy.

Long-grain brown rice: Long-grain brown rice maintains a firm texture after cooking and is common in Indian and western cuisine. Because it is the least starchy of the rice varieties, long-grain does not stick together when cooked.

Medium-grain brown rice: A softer and plumper variety than long-grain, this type of rice is used in cereals and rice cakes. Medium-grain rice is common in Latin and Asian dishes and is often used in soups and side dishes.

Short-grain brown rice: Also known as "sticky rice," short-grain rice is an integral part of Asian meals, including sushi, but most of these products use white rice. It is best to ask for brown rice when dining in Chinese or Japanese restaurants, and if you make sushi at home, prepare it with brown rice.

Sweet rice: Eaten primarily in Japan as part of sushi or dessert, sweet rice, or "mochi rice," is a high-protein, quick-cooking variety. This very sticky rice is nearly translucent when cooked, but again, it is primarily made from white rice, which has been processed and contains few nutrients. Our recipe for brown rice pudding (see page 203) is a healthy alternative to sweet rice for dessert.

Aromatic rice: Texmati, Indian Basmati, and Thai Jasmine are all considered aromatic rice. Grown in Texas, Texmati rice is known for its popcorn-like aroma when cooking. Basmati rice, cultivated in the Himalayas, is a long-grain variety with a mild, nutty flavor, and available in brown basmati rice varieties. Jasmine rice has a sweet and delicate flavor named after its renowned Jasmine fragrance.

Quick-cooking brown rice: This is a precooked variety of brown rice, designed for convenience because it cooks in 10 minutes.

Rice bran oil: Touted for its array of vitamins, minerals, antioxidants, and essential fatty acids, rice bran oil has been shown to lower blood cholesterol levels.

Rice Milk: Used as a substitute for cow's milk or soy milk, rice milk is favored by those who are lactose-intolerant, vegan, or aiming to lose weight. Made by soaking cooked rice in hot water, rice milk is now sold in most commercial grocery stores.

Cooking Rice

If you choose to buy rice sold in bulk, rinse it thoroughly in cool water before preparation to remove any dust or residue. To cook brown rice, pour 1 cup of rice into 2 cups of boiling water or broth. After the liquid returns to a boil, lower the temperature, cover, and simmer for 35-45 minutes. Be sure to cook rice in an amount of water that can be fully absorbed by the rice. If cooked in excess liquid and drained, vital nutrients will be lost with the discarded liquid. To cut the cooking time significantly, soak 1 cup of brown rice in 2 cups of water overnight. Cook the rice in the same water used for soaking. To prevent rice from sticking together, rinse it under cool running water before boiling.

Cooking Ideas: For those who are sensitive to gluten, homemade rice flour is an excellent alternative to traditional white flour. Using a coffee grinder, simply grind uncooked brown rice into a fine powder and use in pancake, cookie, and pastry recipes.

- When preparing wild rice, mix it with any variety of brown rice to add a surprising texture and delicious flavor.
- To make a quick and healthy rice pudding, reheat leftover rice, and add low-fat milk or soymilk, cinnamon, nutmeg, honey, and golden raisins.
- Stir-fry vegetables with shrimp, chicken, or tofu, and serve over leftover brown rice for an instant dinner.

Nutritional Content

An excellent source of carbohydrates, manganese, selenium, phosphorus, magnesium, and B vitamins, rice is truly a nutritional powerhouse. Because brown rice retains its bran layer, it contains four times more insoluble fiber than white rice. Rice is also gluten-free.

Examples of Rice Products

Type of Rice Food	Serving Size	Total Calories	Dietary Fiber (g)
Brown rice, long-grain (cooked)	1 cup	216	3.5
Wild rice (cooked)	1 cup	166	3
Rice noodles (cooked)	1 cup	192	2
Rice cakes, brown rice, unsalted	2 cakes	70	0
Brown rice pudding	⅔ cup	220	1
Rice flour, brown	1 cup	574	7
Rice Krispies cereal	1¼ cup	119	0
Puffed rice cereal	1 cup	56	0

Health Benefits

The scientifically proven benefits of rice have far-reaching effects on health. One serving of brown rice contains 88% of the recommended daily amount of manganese.

Because of its combination of fiber and selenium, eating brown rice on a regular basis may help prevent colon cancer. Fiber minimizes the amount of time that carcinogenic materials spend in contact with colon cells, while selenium has been shown to inhibit the propagation of cancer cells.

For people with elevated cholesterol levels, incorporating brown rice into the diet is a wise decision. Rice bran oil, a component of the rice kernel, has been shown to lower LDL cholesterol. In addition, brown rice raises blood levels of nitric oxide, a molecule known to impede development of plaque in the arteries. Finally, the fiber found in brown rice also lowers cholesterol levels, helps the body maintain stable blood sugar, and prevents gallstone formation.

Rye

German farmers first considered rye to be just a pesky weed growing among the wheat and barley crop. Fortunately, it was not long before they discovered that this stubborn weed, flourishing in the harsh northern climate, had a unique and appealing flavor. Eastern European and Scandinavian countries soon incorporated rye into their daily diets.

Ground mostly into flour for bread, rye remains a staple in many Northern European countries, and it is popular in restaurants across North America. In Finland, rye bread is baked into a flattened disk shape with a hole in the middle. This traditional shape harkens back to a time when breads were strung on horizontal poles beneath farmhouse ceilings for storage. In Germany, traditional rye bread became so common that the word for supper, *Abendbrot*, is literally translated to mean "evening bread." Today, the majority of the world's rye crop is grown in the countries where it naturally thrives: Russia, Canada, Poland, Germany, and Denmark.

Description

Known scientifically as *Secale cereale*, rye bears a slight resemblance to wheat in appearance. Cultivated in varieties ranging from green to brown to yellow, rye is generally found in whole or cracked form. Although it is classified as a "gluten-containing grain," rye's gluten differs from wheat's in that it undergoes a different leavening process, producing more elastic, dense dough. The result is baked goods with a particularly moist, compact, and hearty texture.

When buying rye bread, read ingredient labels carefully to ensure that you are buying bread made of rye flour, not a product made of refined flour and colored with molasses to resemble true rye bread.

Rye berries: Whole rye grains, known as rye berries, are rye in its purest form. Rye berries may be eaten as a cooked cereal or added to flours and multigrain pilaf.

Rye flour: Unlike other grains, the germ and bran of the rye grains are firmly attached to the endosperm. Therefore, even after the milling process, rye flour retains its germ and bran, resulting in a hardy, nourishing flour. Rye flour comes in light, medium, and dark varieties.

Rye flakes: Resembling old-fashioned oats, rye flakes are typically eaten as a hot morning cereal, similar to oatmeal.

Pumpernickel: This dense German sourdough bread is made from a mixture of rye flour and coarsely ground rye meal. The bread also contains molasses, which accounts for the bread's dark color.

Cooking Rye

Before boiling, rinse whole rye under cool, running water. Boil 1 cup of rye in 4 cups of water. Add a pinch of salt then let the combination return to a boil and reduce the heat, letting it simmer for one hour. For softer grains, soak the rye overnight and cook it in the soaking water for several hours.

Cooking Ideas:

- Instead of rice, serve rye berries as a surprising side dish. To prepare, simply sauté the berries in sesame or olive oil, and serve alongside your favorite seafood, poultry, or vegetable dish.
- Whole-rye breads are delicious in deli-style sandwiches.
- Substitute rye flour for wheat flour in any of your favorite recipes.
- Instead of buying crackers and muffins made from refined white flour, look for those made from rye.

Nutritional Content

Rye is an excellent source of manganese, a cofactor for many essential enzymes. In addition, rye is a good source of fiber, selenium, phosphorus,

Examples of Rye Products			
Type of Rye Food	Serving Size	Total Calories	Dietary Fiber (g)
Rye berries, cooked	½ cup	243	12
Rye dinner roll, medium	1 roll	103	2
Rye bread	1 slice	120	2
Pumpernickel bread	1 slice	71	2
Rye flour (dark)	¼ cup	104	7
Rye crackers	4 crackers	120	6

magnesium, and protein. If you have celiac disease or gluten intolerance, rye is not recommended as it contains gluten.

Health Benefits

For diabetics, studies show that rye bread is a smarter choice than whole wheat bread because rye bread does not induce the same insulin response that whole wheat bread does. In a study conducted at the University of Kupio in Finland, researchers compared the consumption of whole-wheat bread with three types of rye bread that varied in their fiber content. By analyzing the insulin response of women who ate each of the four breads, researchers found that whole-wheat bread spiked insulin levels more than all three varieties of rye bread. This study shows that it is not the fiber of rye bread that leads to the stabilized blood sugar, but rather a different component of the rye grain. Further studies are needed to determine the exact mechanism that explains the ability of rye to stabilize insulin response, but scientists hypothesize that the dense starch granules of rye, forming a thick matrix, slow the digestion of rye bread. Slowed digestion leads to a lengthened transformation of starch into sugar, which would account for the steady insulin levels experienced by the research subjects in this study.

For menopausal women, a component of the rye grain may reduce the hot flashes and discomfort associated with reduced levels of estrogen. Rye contains a chemical that acts as a phytoestrogen in the body. Phytoestrogens resemble natural estrogen and have been shown to normalize estrogen activity by mimicking its behavior.

Sorghum

Commonly known as "milo," sorghum has been a staple in Asia and Africa for centuries. Just now making its way into North American kitchens, this tropical grass began its domestication in Ethiopia around 6,000 years ago. Farmers in Africa and India have relied on sorghum for centuries. In the 19th century, sorghum entered into the American mainstream in the form of a syrup sweetener. Cheaper to produce than sugar cane, the "sorghum molasses" became extremely popular. In fact, it was not until the end of the World War I, when it became less expensive to mass-produce refined sugar, that sorghum fell out of favor.

Today, sorghum is the fifth most popular grain in the world and the third leading crop of the United States. Although most of the sorghum grown today is fed to cattle, millions of people worldwide also benefit from the array of nutrients that it has to offer.

Description

Able to withstand drought, the sorghum plant flourishes in harsh climates throughout the world. Although it may be difficult to find in traditional grocery stores, specialty stores that carry African and Indian goods sell a variety of sorghum products, including porridges, breads, and beer.

Cooking Sorghum

Sorghum flour is slightly bland in flavor, making it the perfect flour to combine with other grains. You can easily make gluten-free pizza crusts, breads, and baked goods with sorghum flour. In addition, whole sorghum grains can be prepared similarly to rice: boil 1 cup of sorghum with 2 cups of water and bring to a simmer. Cook until all liquid is absorbed. The resulting dish makes a perfect substitute for rice, pasta, and or any other whole grain dish.

Examples of Sorghum Products

Type of Sorghum Food	Serving Size	Total Calories	Dietary Fiber (g)
Sorghum (whole grain)	¼ cup	163	4
Sorghum syrup	1 tbsp	61	0
Sotghum pilaf	¾ cup	210	5
Sorghum flour (whole grain)	¼ cup	120	3

Nutritional Content

Sorghum is as nutritious as other grains because it is high in fiber, and contains calcium, potassium, phosphorus, iron, and niacin. In addition to carbohydrates, it also contains protein and a small amount of fat.

Health Benefits

Scientific evidence shows that sorghum is closer in its genetic makeup to corn than it is to wheat. Therefore, sorghum is free of gluten and is safe if you have celiac disease and other wheat allergies.

Spelt

Although its exact origins are somewhat mysterious, the history of spelt goes back 5,000 years to its earliest cultivation in Iran and Europe. Spelt's impact was great in ancient times, and it is mentioned in the Bible as one of the seven original grains. At the start of the first millennium, Roman leaders distributed spelt to the poor as part of the world's first known welfare system. As populations migrated westward into Europe, they introduced spelt to new regions, elevating it as an indispensable favorite among Germans, Swiss, and Austrians. During the Middle Ages, spelt gained a new level of popularity when the famous German healer Hildegard von Bingen (St. Hildegard) publicized it as a cure for many illnesses. She wrote: "The spelt is the best of grains. It is rich and nourishing and milder than other grains. It produces a strong body and healthy blood to those who eat it and it makes the spirit of man light and cheerful. If someone is ill boil some spelt, mix it with egg and this will heal him like a fine ointment."

Spelt was introduced to the United States in the 1890s. It was largely replaced by higher-yielding wheat in the 20th century. Because spelt is more hardy that wheat and does not require fertilizer, it began to be promoted by the organic farming movement toward the end of the century.

Description

Known as *Triticum spelta*, spelt is actually a hybrid of emmer and einkorn wheats. It combines the best qualities of these two varieties of wheat, and in some ways, even exceeds them. Unlike wheat, which is grown to lose its husk easily when harvested, spelt retains its sturdy outer husk, protecting the grain from pollutants. The husk also helps spelt to retain its nutrient composition and freshness. Spelt is often described as nutty and sweet in flavor, with a texture that is lighter than that of other whole grains.

Cooking Spelt

The most common way to enjoy spelt is to use its flour as an alternative to whole-wheat or other whole-grain flours. Because spelt does not contain gluten, products made with spelt do not rise evenly and may appear misshapen after baking. Experiment with the amount of liquid used in the recipe or mix spelt flour with gluten-rich flour to obtain better results. Alternatively, look for "light" spelt flour, which is flour made from spelt that has had its bran and germ removed and therefore will produce better results when baking breads.

Cooking Ideas:

- Grind spelt at home into delicious whole-grain flour that can be used any way you would use whole-wheat flour.
- Spelt berries are a flavorful, nutrient-packed alternative to wheat berries and ideal for those with gluten intolerance.
- Rolled spelt flakes are delicious as a hot cereal or as an alternative to oats in oatmeal raisin cookies.

Nutrient Content

When it comes to nutrition, spelt is a true powerhouse. The grain is an excellent source of fiber and B vitamins, and has 10–25% more protein than common wheat. Additionally, spelt contains gluten and may not be appropriate for those with celiac disease or gluten intolerance.

Examples of Spelt Products

Type of Spelt Food	Serving Size	Total Calories	Dietary Fiber (g)
Spelt berries	¼ cup	130	6
Rolled spelt flakes	½ cup	130	3
Spelt flour	¼ cup	120	4
Spelt citrus pilaf	1 cup	190	1
Spelt flatbread	1 flatbread	100	3

Health Benefits

Spelt has high water solubility, allowing its nutrients to be easily absorbed by the body. Spelt is an excellent source of riboflavin (vitamin B_2), a vitamin necessary for proper energy metabolism within cells. Riboflavin may be an important nutrient for migraine sufferers, as it has been found to reduce the frequency of migraine headaches, perhaps by restoring proper energy metabolism in nervous system cells.

Spelt's exceptionally high soluble-fiber content accounts for its positive effects on lowering blood cholesterol and LDL levels. Soluble fiber binds to cholesterol-containing bile in the digestive system and prevents its absorption. The body excretes the excess cholesterol, lowering total blood cholesterol levels and improving the ratio of LDL to HDL cholesterol.

Teff is a tiny grain that is jam-packed with nutrients. In fact, teff is the smallest grain in the world, requiring 150 grains to equal the weight of one grain of wheat. Teff earned its name from the Amharic word for "lost" because its small size made it difficult for farmers to collect during harvest. Originally cultivated in Ethiopia between 4000 and 1000 BC, teff remains a dietary staple in that region.

Engera, an Ethiopian sourdough flat bread made from fermented teff, is eaten throughout the country. Teff has only recently made its way to America: in 1995, an Ethiopian biodiversity project demonstrated teff's ability to thrive without pesticides and fertilizers, attracting the attention of American environmentalists. Today, teff is gaining in popularity and becoming more available in health food and specialty stores.

Description

Teff is a grass characterized by an extensive root system, which allows the plant to flourish in both arid conditions and flooded regions. Variations of teff range in color from white to deep red, brown, or purple. The white varieties of teff impart a mild, nutty flavor that is often compared to the sweetness of chestnuts. Darker varieties have a heartier flavor, similar to hazelnuts.

Cooking Teff

To cook teff place 2 cups water, $^2/_3$ cup teff, and $^1/_2$ teaspoon salt (optional) into a saucepan. Bring to a boil, reduce heat, cover, and simmer for 15 to 20 minutes or until all of the water is absorbed. Remove from heat and let stand in a covered pot for 5 minutes.

Cooking Ideas:

- Use uncooked teff grains as an alternative to sesame seeds or nuts.
- Adding uncooked teff to stews, soups, and casseroles is an excellent way to increase both the flavor and nutritional content of the dish. Simply add the uncooked grain to the dish 30 minutes before serving.
- Add one cup of teff to baking recipes, such as multigrain pancakes, breads, and porridges, for extra flavor and fiber.

Nutritional Content

Teff's small size accounts for its exceptional nutritional density. Because the endosperm is so small, the bulk of the grain is made up of the nutritious bran and germ. Teff is therefore high in fiber, as well as calcium, phosphorus, iron, copper, and thiamin. Its protein is of exceptional quality, with higher lysine (an amino acid) levels than both wheat and barley. Additionally, teff is low in fat and gluten-free, making it a safe and an excellent choice for people with celiac disease and gluten intolerance.

Examples of Teff Products

Type of Teff Food	Serving Size	Total Calories	Dietary Fiber (g)
Teff (cooked)	1 cup	204	8
Teff Moroccan stew	1 cup	380	4

Health Benefits

Because of its notable high fiber content, researchers believe that teff stabilizes blood glucose levels more effectively than other grains. To study this hypothesis, researchers compared the prevalence of diabetes among recent Ethiopian immigrants to that of Ethiopian immigrants who had lived in a Westernized country for at least 30 months. The study took place in Israel, where the diet is comparable to the typical American diet. The study revealed that recent Ethiopian immigrants had diabetes. Among the immigrants living in Israel for at least 30 months, the percentage of those diagnosed with diabetes soared to 8.9%. The researchers attribute the increased rate of diabetes to the elimination of teff, and therefore fiber, from the diet. However, complicating these conclusions is the fact that access to food, and therefore calories, also significantly increased when these immigrants moved to Israel, which may also explain some of the increased rates of diabetes.

Triticale

A biological cross between wheat and rye, triticale was first produced commercially only 80 years ago. The driving force behind the development of a wheat-rye cross was the desire for a high-protein grain that would thrive in areas where wheat production had failed. Triticale's combination of rye's rugged ability to grow in adverse conditions, with wheat's high-protein content and disease resistance, earned it the title "miracle grain" in the 1960s. Ultimately, the efforts proved successful, and today, there are 6 million acres of triticale grown worldwide. China, France, Poland, and Germany produce 90% of the world's supply, which is mainly used to feed animals.

The science behind triticale's development was no simple task: botanists had been working since 1876 to produce a fertile cross of wheat and rye that was comparable to its parent grains in both nutrition and taste. In the 1930s, botanists were overjoyed when they produced a cross that bore seeds. Unfortunately, the diminutive, shriveled seeds failed to grow into a thriving plant. It took several more decades of exacting work and technological advancements to finally produce a viable, hearty grain. Researchers named their cross "triticale" after the scientific names of its parents: wheat (*Triticum*) and rye (*Secale*). Triticale is slowly gaining in popularity and is now used in breads, crackers, porridges, and tortillas in North America.

Description

As triticale is increasing in popularity, more and more health food stores are stocking their shelves with triticale products. One of the more common products available is triticale flour, which is an appropriate, albeit challenging, substitute for wheat flour. Because the gluten in the triticale grain is more delicate than that of wheat, harsh treatment of triticale dough will destroy the fermentation process and lead to unsuccessful results. If you choose to incorporate triticale flour into a bread recipe, knead the dough lightly and allow it to rise only once so it does not interrupt the fermentation process. This will likely result in an exceptionally delicious bread.

In addition to flour, triticale is also available as flakes and berries that make a wonderful addition to any pantry. Triticale flakes make a delicious breakfast cereal when prepared with boiling water and a pinch of salt. Triticale berries, rich and savory in flavor, are perfect as a solo side dish or incorporated into other foods.

Cooking Triticale

To cook whole triticale berries, add $1/3$ cup of berries to 2 cups cold water and soak overnight. When you are ready to cook, add an additional cup of water and bring to a boil. Allow the berries to simmer for 45 minutes. After cooking, refrigerate the berries for 24 hours before serving to allow them to reach their peak of flavor.

Cooking Ideas:
- Substitute triticale flakes for rolled oats in any oatmeal cookie recipe.
- Look for triticale crackers, pancake mixes, and breads at your local health or specialty store.
- Incorporate triticale berries into your favorite rice and barley dishes.
- Try triticale cereal, a hot porridge, for a delightful morning meal.

Nutritional Content

Triticale combines the nutritional highlights of its parent grains, wheat and rye. The grain is low in fat, high in fiber, and is a good source of carbohydrates and protein. Triticale contains gluten and should be avoided by anyone with gluten allergies.

Examples of Triticale Products

Type of Triticale Food	Serving Size	Total Calories	Dietary Fiber (g)
Triticale flour	¼ cup	120	5
Triticale flakes	¼ cup	100	4
Triticale meal (cereal)	¼ cup	120	6
Triticale berries	¼ cup	150	8

Health Benefits

Because of triticale's novelty, this grain has yet to be the feature of any major nutritional study. However, its rich array of nutrients, high fiber content, and similarity to wheat and rye make the incorporation of triticale into your diet an excellent health decision.

Wheat

It is difficult to imagine a world without wheat. Widely hailed as the most important grain in the world, wheat is essential to the daily diets of people around the globe, and it is renowned as the "staff of life." Wheat competes with barley as being the oldest cultivated cereal grain. First cultivated in Western Asia between 8,000 and 10,000 years ago, wheat was largely responsible for man's transition from hunter-gatherer to stationary farmer.

Anthropologists believe that early man first chewed raw wheat kernels, eventually learning to pound the kernels into flour and mix it with water to make porridge. Ancient Greeks, Romans, and Sumerians demonstrated the importance of wheat in their cultures by worshipping gods and goddesses of wheat. In China, ceremonies celebrating wheat date back to at least 2800 BC. The Egyptians prepared the world's first bread from wheat and barley nearly 6,000 years ago. Baked in clay ovens, the bread became the foundation of the ancient Egyptian diet.

Wheat made its way to the New World with Christopher Columbus. For centuries, wheat remained a minor North American crop as it did not fair well in the harsh and variable climate. It was not until a wave of Russian immigrants planted a new variety of wheat, Turkey Red Wheat, in the Kansas flatlands that it began to flourish.

Description

There are six main classes of wheat grown in the United States: red winter, soft red winter, hard red spring, hard white, soft white, and durum. Species of hard wheat provide fine flour that is ideal for baking breads. The high protein content (12–18%) allows hard wheat flour to absorb a significant amount of water, swelling the dough. On the contrary, soft wheat varieties contain less protein (8–11%), making their flours suitable for the production of cakes, cookies, crackers, and cereals.

Refined durum wheat flour: Durum wheat is easily distinguished by its amber-colored kernel and large size. It is the hardiest of all wheat varieties, with a high protein (14–16%) and gluten content which makes it ideal for the production of firm, high-quality pasta products. When durum is milled, the endosperm is coarsely ground into semolina, a granular, golden-colored wheat. Because the milling process robs semolina of its nutrient-rich germ and bran, the flour is enriched with some of the nutrients that have been removed—primarily thiamin, riboflavin, niacin, and folate. The resulting products are low in fiber and lack many of the nutrients naturally found in whole wheat.

Wheat Berries

Whole-wheat flour: Unlike refined durum flour, whole-wheat flours are made by grinding the entire wheat kernel into a fine powder. Since the germ and the bran remain, none of the vitamins, minerals, or fiber are lost in processing. Varieties of whole-wheat flours include whole wheat baking flour, stoneground flour, and graham flour. Quite similar in their nutritional value, these varieties differ in their protein content, which affects the texture of the products made from them. The recipe section in this book includes tips on baking with whole-wheat flour.

Wheat berries: Wheat produces a dry, one-seeded fruit called a caryopsis, more commonly known as a wheat kernel or berry. Wheat berries are hard and vary in color from white to red or purple. The purest form of wheat, wheat berries are available year-round both in raw and dry form or in "ready-to-eat" frozen form.

Bulgur wheat: Bulgur wheat is precooked wheat, typically red winter wheat. Bulgur is made by boiling the wheat kernel and then drying and cracking it into pieces—thus, a portion of the coarse outer bran is removed. This is a quick-cooking form of whole wheat with a rich, nut-like flavor and golden color. Bulgur wheat makes a great dish on its own or is a first-rate companion to meat and poultry dishes. Bulgur comes in three varieties: coarse, medium, and fine. Coarse bulgur is generally cooked like rice and used in pilafs and casseroles; medium bulgur is often used as a breakfast cereal; while fine bulgur is an important ingredient in dishes such as tabbouleh, a classic Middle-Eastern salad.

Cracked wheat: Often confused with bulgur, cracked wheat is made up of raw whole-wheat berries that have been ground into coarse granules, losing a portion of the outer bran. Cracked wheat is not precooked like bulgur wheat. Cracked wheat has a milder flavor than bulgur is available in fine, medium, and coarse varieties, and often used in pilafs and salads.

Cooking Wheat

When cooking with wheat berries, it is important to rinse them first. Once clean, boil 3 cups of water for every 1 cup of wheat berries. Because wheat is so absorbent, one cup of raw berries will yield 2 cups of plump, cooked berries. To cut cooking time in half, soak the wheat berries overnight in the water you intend to cook them in. Wheat berries should be cooked for roughly 25 minutes if presoaked or 45 minutes if they have not been presoaked.

To save even more time, place 1 cup wheat berries in 2 cups water, and microwave on high for 15 to 18 minutes. Watch after 15 minutes that the water does not completely disappear. Strain. Tips on substituting white flour for nutrient-rich, whole-wheat flour are described in detail on page 147.

Cooking Ideas:

- Add a few spoonfuls of wheat germ to yogurt for added flavor.
- Add wheat berries to salads and side dishes.
- When buying bread, rolls, muffins, and crackers, look for "whole-grain wheat" as the first ingredient listed.
- Substitute whole-wheat pasta for white pasta.
- Instead of breadcrumbs, coat chicken or eggplant in bulgur wheat.
- Use whole-wheat flour instead of refined white flour when baking breads, muffins, and even pizza crust.

Nutritional Benefits

Whole wheat contains carbohydrates and boasts an array of nutrients including calcium, iron, B vitamins, magnesium, phosphorus, and other trace elements. Whole wheat is low in fat, contains many essential amino acids, and is an excellent source of dietary fiber.

Health Benefits

For anyone familiar with the pains of constipation, wheat bran may be the cure for your ailments. Studies show that just $1/3$ cup of wheat bran per day will significantly reduce the symptoms of diverticulitis and

Examples of Wheat Products

Type of Wheat Food	Serving Size	Total Calories	Dietary Fiber (g)
Whole-wheat spaghetti (cooked)	1 cup	174	6
Shredded wheat (spoon size) cold cereal	1 cup	167	6
Wheat-germ cereal, ready-to-eat, plain	1 oz (25 g)	108	4
Cream of Wheat, quick, cooked w/ water, no salt	1 cup	129	1
Bread, whole-wheat	1 slice	69	2
English muffin, whole-wheat, toasted	1	135	4
Pancake (4-inch, 10 cm, diameter)	2	184	2
Pretzels, hard, whole-wheat	1	102	2
Crackers, wheat thins	16	130	1
Bulgur (cooked)	1 cup	151	8

chronic constipation. In 89% of patients, symptoms of pain, nausea, flatulence, distension, and constipation were alleviated when wheat bran was added to the diet.

Studies have also shown wheat bran is beneficial in the prevention of colon cancer. People who consumed a substantial amount of wheat bran (28 grams daily) had a significantly lower prevalence of colon polyps compared to those who did not. It is believed that the wheat bran reduces the concentration of the bacterial enzymes and bile acids in the stool that are thought to promote colon cancer.

The insoluble fiber found in wheat bran has also shown to bind to estrogen receptors, an action that may be linked to a decreased risk of breast cancer. The lignans found in whole wheat also reduce blood estrogen levels. Lignans, a type of phytochemical, occupy hormone receptors in the breast, protecting them from receiving too much estrogen. In a recent study, people who ate wheat bran daily for two months showed a 17% decrease in blood estrogen levels. Control groups, eating either corn or oat bran, did not show this decrease.

Chapter 3
Weight-Loss Menus

Transitioning to Whole Grains

If you're like most North Americans, you're probably eating less than one serving of whole grains every day. We know it can seem daunting to get three—or more—servings of whole grains daily, as recommended by the 2005 US Dietary Guidelines, but *The Whole Grain Diet Miracle* can really help. We understand that change does take time, so we have provided the following strategies to help make your transition easier.

Make changes gradually. Start with one additional serving of whole grains for the first week and work your way up to the recommended three servings per day by the end of the sixth week. Breakfast is often a good place to start, since there are numerous whole-grain options available as shown in the following menus in this chapter. In addition to breakfast cereals and various types of regular and low-calorie, whole-wheat and whole-grain breads, you can now find whole-grain bagels, English muffins, frozen waffles, and pancake mixes at the supermarket. Adding a few spoonfuls of whole-grain granola to a cup of yogurt can serve as either breakfast or a snack. Our recipe for parfait with cinnamon oat granola includes directions on how to make nutritious, homemade granola (see page 155).

Be sure to drink enough water. Adding fiber to your diet in the form of whole grains adds bulk to your stool. To keep it soft and moving, it is important to drink enough water to prevent bloating and constipation. Water also helps your digestive system work more efficiently, and most experts recommend drinking at least six to eight glasses a day.

Make substitutions, not additions. Don't go overboard when introducing whole grains, or you'll be adding too many calories along with your grains. Pay close attention to the serving sizes in all our recipes, such as two pancakes, 1 cup of rice pilaf, or 1 cup of teff Moroccan stew (see page 185). We provide the nutritional analysis for each recipe, which gives you an idea of how many calories you're getting for each serving. If you already nibble on crackers between meals, it's fine to swap whole-grain ones for your usual refined ones. But, topping off a meal with whole-grain oatmeal cookies when you don't usually indulge probably won't help you to lose weight.

Keep it simple. People often think of whole-grain foods as exotic or a lot of work to prepare. But grocery store shelves are burgeoning with easy-to-use packaged foods that are familiar and quick to make. Whole-wheat spaghetti doesn't take any longer to cook than regular pasta, and even some frozen dinners now offer brown rice instead of white. All of our 50 recipes are no hassle to prepare, because they use readily available ingredients. We have tried to keep them as simple as possible and many can be prepared in advance.

Go for variety. Forcing yourself to eat the same "healthy" cereal every day can get really boring after a while. So, take advantage of the wide variety of whole-grain products now available. Try our delicious amaranth grits (page 149) instead of your usual grits. Rather than going for the instant brands, make old-fashioned oatmeal with low-fat milk, raisins, and a few tablespoons of unprocessed oat bran. Instead of your usual boxed pancake mix, you can also substitute our homemade buckwheat blueberry pancakes (page 150). Add quinoa to your old stand-by tuna sandwich and buy spelt to make the salads from our recipe section. You'll taste the difference.

Move out of your comfort zone. Once you feel comfortable swapping some familiar foods for whole-grain versions, consider branching out. Try bulgar, buckwheat, quinoa, spelt, and millet. These make great side dishes, or they can be added to soups, salads, main dishes, and even desserts, as shown in Chapter 4. Because there is such variety of vitamins, minerals, antioxidants, and phytochemicals in all the grains, eating all of these whole grains on a regular basis will ensure that you get the greatest benefit.

Make over your recipes. Swapping whole-wheat or rye flour for white flour in recipes is one easy way to work some whole grains into your diet. If a recipe calls for all-purpose flour, you can substitute whole-wheat flour for half of that amount. For example, if your recipe says to add 2 cups of all-purpose flour, add 1 cup of all-purpose and make the other cup whole-wheat flour. (Substituting the entire amount of all-purpose flour for whole-wheat flour may result in lower volume and coarser texture in baked goods.) Or, when baking for the holidays, you can add old-fashioned oats to the topping on pies or crisps. See the introduction to the recipe section on page 146 for direction of how to make the transition to more whole-grain products when baking.

It's the little things. Even small changes make a big difference in the long run, so keep this in mind if you get frustrated. Incorporating more whole grains into your meals and snacks is a lifestyle change, which takes time. Look for small ways to add more whole grains into your diet, such as swapping your regular salad croutons for whole-wheat ones. And remember, many of our whole-grain recipes are considered two servings of whole grains. For example, a quinoa tuna sandwich (page 174) made with two slices of whole-wheat bread or 1 cup of millet butternut squash soup (page 159) both count as two servings.

Encouraging Kids to Eat Whole Grains

Getting children to eat whole-grain foods may seem like a challenge. We often assume that they will only be satisfied with soft, white bread made from refined grains and fear that they will turn up their noses at anything healthy. But, with so many new products showing up on supermarket shelves and even in restaurants, getting whole grains into your child's diet is easier than ever.

The number of whole-grain options for kids is skyrocketing. Familiar foods, such as cereals and pasta are now available in whole-grain versions, making it easier to entice children into making the switch. And with more whole-grain options in the snack and baking aisles, your kids can have their way and get whole grains, too. Here are some ideas to help you get started.

Start early. Once your infant has tolerated dry rice cereal with iron, transition him or her to other flavors such as barley and oat infant cereals, this should occur by seven months. By age two, they may even go for our amaranth grits recipe on page 149.

Finger food. Toddlers who are just beginning finger foods will often happily gobble up whatever you put in front of them—or even what's on your plate. So, go ahead and make some of those items whole grain.

Try bite-size pieces of whole-wheat toast, buckwheat pancakes, brown rice cakes, cooked whole-wheat pasta, or whole-grain O's cereal. Little ones won't notice the difference, and they'll be used to the taste and texture by the time you move on to more advanced foods.

Start small. If whole grains are new to your crew, don't try to make over your whole pantry in one shopping trip. Choose one or two foods you think your kids might be willing to try and gradually transition from there. If they like cinnamon raisin swirl bread or English muffins, for example, try one of the new whole-grain versions, or pack them a granola bar with whole oats instead of a cereal bar made from refined flour. Since most kids like pasta, make a medley of whole wheat and white pasta or begin with whole-grain rather than whole-wheat pasta products. These taste great and are preferred by children.

Go with what you know. Before introducing exotic new grains, like spelt or quinoa, to the family table, try whole-grain versions of products your kids already know and love. Many old standbys of the cereal aisle, even the most kid-friendly, are now labeled as "made with 100% whole grains." But, watch out for the sugar content and try to select cereals with less than 5 grams of sugar per serving. Also, try frozen whole-wheat waffles or whole-wheat pita bread, bagels, and hamburger buns. Whole-wheat macaroni and cheese is available in health food stores and will hopefully become a standard item in your local supermarkets. And of course, let kids enjoy their old-time favorite pizza—just go for the whole-grain crust and try our kamut pizza on page 179, which has been gobbled up by kids.

Use the hunger window. Kids of all ages are much more likely to try new foods when they are really hungry. This may be at breakfast, or after school for toddlers and children. Teenagers who are active with sports may need a snack before, during, or after practice and games. So take advantage of these times and offer whole-grain varieties as much as possible.

Attack the snacks. Active kids need refueling between meals, but many snack foods are high in salt and sugar. So, try swapping your child's potato or tortilla chips for pita chips made from whole wheat or rye. Other good choices include whole-grain crackers, popcorn, or mini rice cakes. Serve these with a ½ cup, low-fat yogurt or cut up fresh fruit such as apples, grapes, or bananas, and they'll be back for more the next day.

Wrap it up. Wraps are all the rage these days, but most are made with refined flour. Try substituting whole-wheat wraps, and corn or sprouted grain tortillas for your kids' tacos, sandwiches, and quesadillas — with enough tasty fillings, they probably won't notice the difference. And if you let them help make their own wraps and teach them how to roll them up, they will be more likely to eat this healthy sandwich.

Don't deprive them. When it comes to sweets, whole grains are moving out of the organic aisle and into the mainstream. You can now find brand-name chocolate-chip cookies and fig bars made with whole wheat right next to the standard versions. Oatmeal cookies are another good choice, but make sure they contain whole, rather than refined, oats (see recipe on page 201).

Meet them halfway. If your family is reluctant to make the switch to whole grains, take baby steps. Make a sandwich with white bread on top and whole wheat on the bottom. Or sneak a small amount of whole-grain flour into recipes that call for white flour, such as pancakes or muffins. Our buckwheat blueberry pancakes are sure to be a big hit with kids (see recipe on page 150). Try our oat-bran banana walnut muffins (page 154) and use a mini-muffin tin, which makes 24 muffins instead of 12, which kids find very appealing when baking.

Think outside the box. Whole-grain options don't have to be limited to the pre-packaged products currently on store shelves. Make your own whole-wheat bread crumbs in the blender to use as a coating for baked chicken or your own home-made chicken nuggets. Our quinoa tuna salad sandwich is also another excellent choice for children's challenging palates (see recipe on page 174).

Hit the books. Check out one of the many cookbooks for children now available and enlist your family's help in choosing what's on the menu. Cute recipe names and colorful pictures add to the fun and help kids feel more excited about trying something new. Make a list of the healthy ingredients together and take them with you to the supermarket to search for these items. It will seem like a treasure hunt, and will also prove to be a great educational opportunity.

Let them help cook. Give the kids an apron and spoon and put them to work. Getting involved in meal preparation is a great way for both children and teenagers to learn about what they eat, and they will be much more likely to try new foods if they have cooked it themselves. In this book we provide 50 delicious, kid-friendly recipes, so ask your family to select the ones they want to help you prepare. Bon Appetit!

Top 10 Rules for the 2-Week Jumpstart Session

1 No drinking alcohol for two weeks during the jump-start menus.

2 No skipping meals, especially when you are working, running around on the weekends with the family, or traveling.

3 Eat on a schedule, at similar times each day, for example, breakfast between 7 and 9AM, lunch between 12 noon and 1PM, and dinner between 5 and 7PM.

4 Try to eat at least 2 cups of fruit and 2½ cups of vegetables every day.

5 Listen to your stomach. Eat when you are hungry, and stop eating before you feel full. Also try to eat slowly and enjoy your meals and snacks.

6 At home, eat sitting down at the kitchen table with the television turned off.

7 Limit television viewing (as well as other sedentary activities) to 1 hour per day and avoid eating in front of the television.

8 Take a multivitamin supplement every day to ensure you are getting all the nutrients your body needs.

9 Consider taking a calcium supplement—and drink calcium-enriched products—to reach your daily requirements (men and women 19–50 years = 1000 mg/day, 51+ years = 1200 mg/day).

10 Make 3 hours of exercise each week your goal. Based on what you do now, start slow and increase gradually. Begin by walking and taking the stairs more often.

WEEK ONE	Monday	Tuesday	Wednesday
Breakfast	1 oat-bran banana walnut muffin (p154) 1 tsp lite margarine 1 cup 1% milk	1 cup oatmeal made with 1% milk 2 tb raisins 1 cup herbal tea	1 slice low-calorie whole-grain toast 1 tb almond butter 1 tb all-fruit jam 1 cup 1% milk
Snack	1 cup low-fat yogurt 2 tb raisins 1 cup water	1 apple 2 tb unsalted nuts 1 cup water	1 slice low-calorie, whole-grain toast 2 tb fat-free cottage or ricotta cheese 1 cup water
Lunch	1¼ cups barley and mushroom soup (p158) 6 whole-grain crackers diet beverage or 1 cup water	1 quinoa and tuna sandwich on low-calorie, whole-wheat bread (p174) with sliced tomato 1 tb lite mayo diet beverage	1 cup amaranth chicken salad (p160) 6 spelt crackers diet beverage or 1 cup water
Dinner	6 oz (175 g) grilled salmon ¾ cup brown rice steamed string beans with almonds garden salad 2 tb low-fat dressing 1 cup water	1¼ cup Louisiana-style red beans and spelt (p184) steamed green and red peppers 1 cup water	1 cup whole-wheat pasta with capers, tomatoes, and mushroom sauce garden salad 2 tb low-fat dressing 1 cup water
Dessert or Snack	3 kiwi fruits decaf diet drink	1 slice melon decaf diet drink	2 oatmeal raisin cookies (p201) decaf diet drink

130

Thursday	Friday	Saturday	Sunday
1 oatmeal breakfast bar ½ grapefruit ½ cup low-fat, fruited yogurt	1 cup whole-grain cereal 1 cup 1% milk 1 fresh peach ½ cup vegetable juice	2 buckwheat blueberry pancakes (p150) 2 tb maple syrup ½ cup orange juice	Vegetable omelet (2 eggs) 1 slice low-calorie, whole-wheat toast 2 soy or vegetarian sausages ½ cup orange juice
1 cup low-sugar, whole-grain cereal 1 cup 1% milk 1 cup water	1 hard-boiled egg 6 whole-grain crackers 1 tb lite mayo 1 cup water	1 puffed corn cake 1 tb peanut butter ½ banana 1 cup water	1 low-fat cheese stick 2 kiwis 1 cup water
¾ cup lemon bulgur salad (p163) field greens 2 tb low-fat dressing diet beverage or 1 cup water	1 cup buckwheat noodle, artichoke, and tofu salad (p162) diet beverage or 1 cup water	1 cup toasted corn and bulgur salad (p164) 1 slice rye bread diet beverage or 1 cup water	4 oz (100 g) turkey breast burger in whole-wheat wrap with mustard sauce 2 sliced tomatoes diet beverage or 1 cup water
6 oz (175 g) grilled Mahi Mahi with peppers, onion, and tomato 1 cup millet mashers (p190) steamed spinach 1 cup water	6 oz (175 g) grilled chicken breast ¾ cup farro risotto (p189) steamed zucchini 1 cup water	6 oz (175 g) blackened catfish 1 cup kale with quinoa and sesame (p191) steamed peas and carrots 1 cup water	4 oz (100 g) filet mignon 2 oatcakes with goat cheese (p173) sliced tomatoes and avacado steamed broccoli 1 cup water
½ cup fresh berries ½ cup low-fat yogurt decaf diet drink	1 nectarine decaf diet drink	2 cups air-popped popcorn decaf diet drink	1 sliced peach ½ cup low-fat yogurt decaf diet drink

131

WEEK TWO

	Monday	Tuesday	Wednesday
Breakfast	1 yogurt parfait with cinnamon-oat granola (p155) ½ cup orange juice	3 scrambled egg whites 2 tb salsa 1 slice low-cal, whole-wheat toast 1 tsp lite margarine ½ cup orange juice	1 buckwheat crepe with ham and low-fat cheese (p151) ½ grapefruit 1 cup 1% milk
Snack	1 puffed corn cake 1 tb almond butter ½ banana 1 cup water	1 apple 6 whole-grain crackers 1 cup water	1 whole-grain cereal bar 1 cup 1% milk
Lunch	1 cup quinoa and fresh baby spinach salad (p165) 6 whole-grain crackers diet beverage or 1 cup water	3 Middle-Eastern bulgur meatballs (p178) carrot and celery sticks 2 tb low-fat dressing diet beverage or 1 cup water	2 amaranth zucchini-squash patties (p169) 1 cup millet and butternut squash soup (p159) diet beverage
Dinner	1½ cups veal stew with millet (p180) sliced cucumbers 2 tb low-fat dressing 1 cup water	1½ cups shrimp soba primavera (p183) garden salad 2 tb low-fat dressing 1 cup water	6 oz (175 g) grilled chicken ¾ cup sorghum and pinenut pilaf steamed string beans 1 cup water
Dessert or Snack	1 low-fat cheese stick and 4 whole-grain crackers decaf diet drink	2 cups air-popped popcorn decaf diet drink	1 cup low-fat yogurt 1 cup fresh berries decaf diet drink

Thursday	Friday	Saturday	Sunday
1 cup whole-grain cereal 1 cup 1% milk ½ banana 1 cup herbal tea	1 cup oatmeal made with 1% milk 2 tb dried cranberries ½ cup orange juice	2 slices whole-grain French toast (p156) 2 tb maple syrup 1 cup 1% milk	1 scrambled egg 1 cup southwestern corn and red potato hash browns (p152) ½ cup vegetable juice
½ cup fat-free cottage cheese 6 whole-grain crackers 1 cup water	2 plums 1 cup low-fat yogurt 1 cup water	2 clementine oranges 1 cup water	1 cup low-fat yogurt ½ cup raisins 1 cup water
1 cup triticale berries and roasted Asian eggplant salad (p167) 1 slice millet banana bread (p197) diet beverage	1 quinoa-stuffed pepper with ground turkey (p182) 1 sliced tomato diet beverage or 1 cup water	1 quinoa tuna salad sandwich on whole-wheat bread (p174) lettuce and tomato diet beverage or 1 cup water	¾ cup Grecian spelt, cucumber, dill, and mint salad (p166) diet beverage or 1 cup water
1 slice sweet tomato-glazed veggie loaf (p181) sliced tomato, avocado, onion, and basil salad steamed broccoli 1 cup water	6 oz (175 g) grilled tuna 1 cup millet and butternut squash soup (p159) 6 sesame-seed kamut crackers 1 cup water	6 oz (175 g) pork loin ¾ cup lemon bulgur salad with chickpeas (p163) garden salad 2 tb low-fat dressing 1 cup water	1 cup teff Moroccan stew (p185) 1 cup buckwheat and bell pepper saute (p188) steamed spinach 1 cup water
1 cup strawberries (fresh or frozen) decaf diet drink	2 plums decaf diet drink	1 slice nutty millet banana bread (p197) decaf diet drink	1 slice pear crisp (p202) 2 tb fat-free, whipped topping decaf diet drink

Top 10 Rules for the 4-Week Everyday Menus

1 Keep alcohol intake to one drink per day. One drink is a 12-ounce (355 ml) beer, 6-ounce (177 ml) glass of wine, or 1-ounce (30 ml) hard liquor.

2 Concentrate on eating smaller portions in all settings, especially for lunch and dinner.

3 Use smaller plates, put less food on your plate, avoid seconds, and see how full you feel.

4 Eat only until you are satisfied rather than full, especially when you are eating in a restaurant. Refer to the eating out section on page 205 for how to incorporate whole grains into those menus.

5 Try to share an entrée when eating out. Order a salad, and one appetizer and one entrée, for two people. If you are eating alone, ask for half an order or lunch portions to prevent overeating.

6 Incorporate sugar-free beverages into your diet to reduce your total caloric intake.

7 Always trim the fat from your meats and poultry before cooking and remove the skin from poultry before eating.

8 Use nonstick vegetable spray and nonstick pans when cooking to reduce the need for extra calories.

9 Use fresh and dried herbs for seasoning when cooking. Avoid using the salt shaker.

10 Aim for three servings of low-fat dairy every day. If you cannot tolerate milk products, try lactose-free milk or soymilk. Both now come enriched with calcium.

WEEK THREE

	Monday	Tuesday	Wednesday
Breakfast	¾ cup amaranth grits (p149) 1 scrambled egg with low-fat cheese ½ cup vegetable juice	1 cup oatmeal made with 1% milk 2 tb raisins ½ cup grapefruit juice	1 yogurt parfait with cinnamon-oat granola (p155) ½ cup orange juice
Snack	1 apple 1 cup water	sliced cucumbers, tomatoes, and celery 2 tb hummus dip 1 cup water	1 cup sliced peaches ½ cup low-fat cottage cheese 1 cup water
Lunch	1¼ cups Italian barley, escarole, and turkey sausage (p177) 1 fresh pear diet beverage or 1 cup water	1 cup toasted corn and bulgur salad (p164) 1 cup millet butternut squash soup (p159) diet beverage or 1 cup water	1½ cups buckwheat noodle, artichoke, and tofu salad (p162) garden salad 2 tb low-fat dressing diet beverage or 1 cup water
Dinner	4 oz (100 g) grilled chicken 1 cup whole-wheat pasta with red sauce field greens 2 tb low-fat dressing 1 cup water	4 oz (100 g) sirloin steak 2 buckwheat crepes with goat cheese and sun-dried tomatoes (p170) steamed zucchini 1 cup water	6 oz (175 g) grilled tilapia 1 cup triticale berries and roasted Asian eggplant salad (p167) steamed spinach 1 cup water
Dessert or Snack	6 grapes 1 cup low-fat yogurt decaf diet drink	1 orange decaf diet drink	1 slice chocolate peanut butter pie (p200) decaf diet drink

Thursday	Friday	Saturday	Sunday
1 oat-bran banana walnut muffin (p154) 1 hard-boiled egg 1 cup 1% milk	1 cup low-sugar, whole-grain cereal 1 fresh peach 1 cup 1% milk	1 corn huevos rancheros (p153) ½ cup southwestern hash browns (p152) ½ grapefruit 1 cup 1% milk	2 buckwheat blueberry pancakes (p150) 2 tb maple syrup 1 cup 1% milk
1 cup low-fat yogurt 1 cup fresh berries 1 cup water	1 small banana ¼ cup unsalted almonds 1 cup water	1 hard-boiled egg 6 whole-grain crackers 1 tb lite mayo 1 cup water	1 rice cake 1 tb peanut butter 1 apple 1 cup water
2 cups barley, corn, and arugula salad (p161) steamed cauliflower diet beverage or 1 cup water	1 quinoa and tuna sandwich on low-calorie, whole-wheat bread (p174) 1 tb lite mayo diet beverage or 1 cup water	2 oatmeal oven chicken fingers (p172) 1 slice southwestern cornbread (p196) steamed Swiss chard diet beverage or 1 cup water	1 cup amaranth chicken salad (p160) field greens 1 cup fresh berries 1 cup water
1½ cups shrimp soba primavera (p183) green salad 2 tb low-fat dressing 1 cup water	2 slices kamut, spinach, and goat cheese pizza (p179) garden salad 2 tb low-fat dressing 1 cup water	6 oz (175 g) grilled chicken breast ¾ cup farro risotto (p189) steamed peas 1 cup water	2 BBQ shrimp kebabs 1 cup spelt citrus-pistachio pilaf (p194) steamed asparagus 1 cup water
1 cup air-popped popcorn decaf diet drink	1 sliced melon decaf drink	3 kiwi fruits decaf diet drink	1 buckwheat brownie (p199) 1 cup 1% milk

WEEK FOUR	Monday	Tuesday	Wednesday	
Breakfast	1 slice whole-grain French toast (p156) 1 tb maple syrup 1 cup 1% milk	1 cup oatmeal made with 1% milk 2 tb dried apricots 1 cup herbal tea	1 slice southwestern cornbread (p196) 1 hard-boiled egg 1 cup 1% milk	
Snack	3 kiwi fruits 1 cup water	1 apple 2 tb unsalted almonds 1 cup water	1 cup low-fat yogurt ½ cup fresh berries 1 cup water	
Lunch	4 oz (100 g) grilled chicken breast ¾ cup barley with leeks and fennel (p187) diet beverage or 1 cup water	1 cup triticale berries and roasted Asian eggplant salad (p167) 1 cup millet butternut squash soup (p159) diet beverage or 1 cup water	1 quinoa tuna salad sandwich on low-calorie, whole-wheat bread (p174) lettuce and tomato diet beverage or 1 cup water	
Dinner	1 quinoa-stuffed pepper (p182) field greens 2 tb low-fat dressing steamed snow peas 1 cup water	3 Middle-Eastern bulgur meatballs (p178) 1 cup whole-wheat pasta with red sauce field greens 2 tb low-fat dressing diet beverage or 1 cup water	1 cup teff Moroccan stew (p185) ½ cup spelt citrus-pistachio pilaf (p194) steamed spinach 1 cup water	
Dessert or Snack	1 ripe mango 1 cup low-fat yogurt decaf diet drink	½ fat-free sorbet decaf diet drink	2 oatmeal raisin cookies (p201) decaf diet drink	

Thursday	Friday	Saturday	Sunday
1 slice nutty millet banana bread (p197) 1 tb peanut butter 1 cup 1% milk	1 yogurt parfait with cinnamon-oat granola (p155) 1 cup water	¾ cup amaranth grits (p149) 2 scrambled egg whites with tomatoes ½ cup orange juice	1 buckwheat crepe with ham and cheese (p151) 1 cup 1% milk
1 low-fat cheese stick ½ grapefruit 1 cup water	1 cup low-sugar, whole-grain cereal 1 cup 1% milk	1 banana 1 cup 1% milk	1 rice cake 1 tb peanut butter 1 cup water
2 buckwheat crepes with goat cheese and sun-dried tomatoes (p170) 1 cup low-fat yogurt diet beverage or 1 cup water	1¼ cups barley and mushroom soup (p158) 2 amaranth-zucchini squash patties (p169) diet beverage or 1 cup water	1 slice sweet tomato-glazed veggie loaf (p181) sliced cucumber, tomato, and basil salad 1 cup water	1 open-faced, chicken-salad sandwich on 1 slice rye bread (p198) carrot sticks 1 cup low-fat yogurt diet beverage
4 oz (100 g) grilled sirloin 1 cup millet mashers (p190) steamed fennel and cauliflower 1 cup water	sesame amaranth and salmon with zucchini and broccoli (p176) steamed red and green peppers 1 cup water	1 cup quinoa and fresh baby spinach salad (p165) 2 oat cakes with goat cheese and dried plums (p173) 1 cup water	3 lamb chops 1 herbed bulgur stuffed tomato (p171) ¾ cup Grecian spelt and mint salad (p166) 1 cup water
1 cup berries 2 tb fat-free whipped topping decaf diet drink	1 orange decaf diet drink	1 apple 1 cup low-fat yogurt decaf diet drink	1 slice chocolate peanut butter pie (p200) decaf diet drink

WEEK FIVE

	Monday	Tuesday	Wednesday
Breakfast	1 cup oatmeal made with 1% milk 2 tb almonds ½ cup orange juice	1 scrambled egg with 1 tb salsa 1 cup southwestern corn and red potato hash browns (p152) ½ cup vegetable juice	1 cup low-sugar, whole-grain cereal 1 fresh peach 1 cup 1% milk
Snack	1 low-fat cheese stick 1 cup water	2 tb unsalted almonds 1 cup low-fat yogurt 1 cup water	10 sliced cucumbers 2 tb hummus dip 1 cup water
Lunch	¾ cup lemon bulgur salad (p163) 1 sliced tomato 1 slice rye bread (p198) diet beverage or 1 cup water	2 cornmeal-crusted chicken fingers (p172) 1 slice southwestern cornbread (p196) diet beverage or 1 cup water	1 cup millet and butternut squash soup (p159) 1 slice millet banana bread (p197) 1 tsp lite margarine or 1 cup water
Dinner	4 oz (100 g) grilled chicken 1 cup sorghum bell pepper pilaf (p193) 1 slice whole-wheat bread 1 cup water	6 oz (175 g) grilled tuna ¾ cup curried squash risotto (p192) steamed string beans 1 cup water	2 slices kamut pizza with spinach and goat cheese (p179) garden salad 2 tb low-fat dressing 1 cup water
Dessert or Snack	2 oatmeal raisin cookies (p201) decaf diet drink	2 cups fresh watermelon slices decaf diet drink	1 cup pineapple slices decaf diet drink

Thursday	Friday	Saturday	Sunday
1 whole-grain corn huevos rancheros (p153) ½ grapefruit 1 cup 1% milk	1 cup oatmeal made with 1% milk 1 tb maple syrup ½ cup orange juice	1 buckwheat crepe with ham and cheese (p151) 1 cup 1% milk	2 slices whole-grain French toast (p156) 2 tb maple syrup 1 cup 1% milk
1 low-fat cheese stick 1 apple 1 cup water	1 cup fat-free yogurt ½ cup berries 1 cup water	carrots and celery sticks 2 tb fat-free dressing 1 cup water	2 clementine oranges 1 cup water
1 cup kale with quinoa and sesame (p191) diet beverage or 1 cup water	1 cup buckwheat noodle, artichoke, and tofu salad (p162) diet beverage or 1 cup water	1 quinoa-stuffed pepper with ground turkey (p182) field greens 2 tb low-fat dressing diet beverage	1 cup toasted corn and bulgur salad (p164) 1 slice rye bread (p198) diet beverage or 1 cup water
6 oz (175 g) grilled Mahi Mahi 1 cup sorghum and bell pepper pilaf (p193) 1 cup barley, corn, and arugula salad (p161) 1 cup water	1¼ cups veal stew with millet and carrots (p180) ¾ cup farro risotto (p189) 1 cup water	1½ cups shrimp soba primavera (p183) 1 herbed bulgur-stuffed tomato (p171) steamed zucchini 1 cup water	1¼ cups Italian barley with escarole, and turkey sausage (p177) field greens 2 tb low-fat dressing 1 cup water
2 cups low-fat yogurt decaf diet drink	fresh apricot, nectarine, and peach salad decaf diet drink	¾ cup brown-rice pudding (p203) decaf diet drink	apple slices topped with low-fat yogurt and granola decaf diet drink

WEEK SIX

	Monday	Tuesday	Wednesday
Breakfast	1 cup low-sugar, whole-grain cereal 1 small sliced banana 1 cup 1% milk	1 yogurt parfait with cinnamon-oat granola (p155) ½ cup orange juice	1 cup oatmeal made with 1% milk 2 tb raisins 1 tb maple syrup ½ cup orange juice
Snack	puffed corn cake 1 tb almond butter 1 orange 1 cup water	2 whole-grain fig cookies 1 cup water	1 cup fruit cocktail in own juice 1 cup water
Lunch	3 Middle-Eastern meatballs (p178) 1 cup whole-wheat pasta with red sauce field greens 2 tb low-fat dressing diet beverage	1¼ cups barley and mushroom soup (p158) 6 kamut crackers diet beverage or 1 cup water	2 amaranth-zucchini squash patties (p169) 1 cup millet and butternut squash soup (p159) diet beverage or 1 cup water
Dinner	6 oz (175 g) grilled salmon 1 cup barley with leeks and fennel (p187) steamed asparagus 1 cup water	1 cup teff Moroccan stew (p185) sliced tomato, onion, and avocado salad steamed peas and carrots 1 cup water	1 slice sweet tomato-glazed veggie loaf (p181) 1 cup quinoa and baby spinach salad (p165) 1 cup water
Dessert or Snack	1 cup fat-free sorbet decaf diet drink	1 cup sliced peaches ½ cup plain yogurt decaf diet drink	1 slice nutty millet banana bread (p197) decaf diet drink

Thursday	Friday	Saturday	Sunday
1 slice low-calorie, whole-grain toast 1 tb almond butter ½ grapefruit 1 cup 1% milk	1 whole-grain corn huevos rancheros (p153) 1 cup southwestern hash browns (p152) 1 cup 1% milk	2 buckwheat blueberry pancakes (p150) 2 tb maple syrup ½ banana 1 cup 1% milk	¾ cup amaranth grits (p149) 2 scrambled eggs 1 slice low-salt ham ½ cup orange juice
½ cup low-fat yogurt 1 cup water	1 apple 1 cup water	carrots and celery sticks 2 tb hummus dip 1 cup water	1 low-fat cheese stick 1 pear 1 cup water
1½ cups Louisiana-style red beans and spelt (p184) steamed carrots and broccoli diet beverage or 1 cup water	1 cup sesame amaranth and salmon with zucchini and broccoli (p176) diet beverage or 1 cup water	2 buckwheat crepes with goat cheese and sun-dried tomatoes (p170) diet beverage or 1 cup water	1 herbed bulgur-stuffed tomato (p171) sliced carrots and cucumbers diet beverage or 1 cup water
2 oven–fried chicken fingers (p172) 1 slice southwestern cornbread (p196) steamed collard greens 1 cup water	4 oz (100 g) filet mignon ½ cup spelt citrus-pistachio pilaf (p194) steamed string beans with sliced almonds	2 slices kamut pizza with spinach and goat cheese (p179) garden salad 2 tb low-fat dressing 1 cup water	6 oz (175 g) broiled turkey breast 1 cup triticale berries with roasted Asian eggplant salad (p167) steamed zucchini and red peppers 1 cup water
1 buckwheat brownie (p199) decaf diet drink	1 slice pear crisp (p202) decaf diet drink	1 cup fresh berries decaf diet drink	2 whole-grain fig cookies decaf diet drink

143

Chapter 4
The Recipes

Cooking and Baking with Whole Grain Flours

All–Purpose Flour: All-purpose flour is used to make yeast breads, cakes, cookies, and pastries. Unfortunately, this flour is processed, removing much of the flour's nutrient content. Although the refined product is typically enriched, you can substitute portions of all-purpose flour with whole-grain flours to replenish the nutrient composition. All-purpose flour is made from wheat and is not safe for people allergic to gluten.

Amaranth: Amaranth flour is 100% stone-ground, a process that maintains the nutrient content of the grain. In baked goods, replace ¼ of all-purpose flour with amaranth flour, which doesn't contain gluten.

Barley: Sweet and nutty in flavor, barley flour is ideal for creating moist biscuits, pancakes, and breads. Substitute ⅓ cup of barley flour for regular flour. Barley is not safe for people allergic to gluten.

Buckwheat: Because of its delicately nutty flavor, buckwheat is ideal for use in pancakes, pie crusts, breads, and even brownies. Simply combine buckwheat flour with whole-wheat flour. Pure buckwheat does not contain gluten, however, mixing buckwheat with whole-wheat or all-purpose flour will introduce gluten into the mixture.

Corn: Corn flour is perfect for bread, muffin, and biscuit recipes— simply replace cornmeal for moister baked goods. Corn is gluten-free.

Kamut: Kamut flour is rich and buttery in flavor. Replace half of all-purpose flour with kamut flour. Kamut contains gluten.

Millet: Millet flour is a perfect alternative for all-purpose white flour.

Replace ¼ cup millet flour for unbleached white flour and enrich your baked goods with vitamins and minerals without changing the flavor. Millet is gluten-free.

Oats: Oat flour is delicious in cookies, pancakes, and muffins. Oats are typically grown in wheat fields and, although they do not contain gluten, they are not recommended for people who are allergic to gluten.

Rice: Brown-rice flour is perfect for baking delicate breads and pizza crust. Look for products that are 100% stoneground, which will be finer in texture. Brown rice is gluten-free.

Rye: Dark rye flour is the ultimate ingredient for dense rye breads. Light rye flour (unbleached) is made by removing the bran and germ of the rye berry, creating a lighter bread. Rye contains gluten.

Spelt: Spelt flour can be used in the same manner as whole-wheat flour for all of your baking needs. Like wheat, spelt is a gluten-grain.

Teff: Teff flour is light in flavor and texture. To use, substitute teff for ¼ of all-purpose flour. Teff does not contain gluten.

Triticale: Triticale flour can be used to make yeast breads without using traditional wheat. When making bread with triticale, be sure to cut the kneading time in half as to not disrupt the delicate fermentation process. Most triticale breads require 5 to 10 minutes of extra cooking time. Because triticale is closely related to wheat, it contains gluten.

Wheat: Whole-wheat flour is one of the most versatile flours available, offering a variety of nutrients along with delicious flavor. To boost the nutrient content of your baked goods, replace half of all-purpose flour with whole-wheat flour. Substituting the entire amount of all-purpose flour may result in baked goods with lower volume and coarser texture. This flour is not appropriate for anyone allergic to gluten.

Breakfast

Amaranth "Grits"

Makes about 4½ cups. Serves 6

If you're from the southern states, you'll know that this dish is not any ordinary grits. But, this recipe is a keeper (for northerners, too) as something rather extraordinary, a great way to try amaranth for the first time.

3 cups reduced-sodium chicken broth
¾ cup fat-free half-n-half
1 tablespoon unsalted butter or trans-free
    margarine
1 cup amaranth
⅛ teaspoon fine sea salt, or to taste
⅛ teaspoon freshly ground white pepper,
    or to taste
2 tablespoons minced fresh chives (optional)

Nutrition Analysis (¾ cup)
Calories: 170
Calories From Fat: 35
Total Fat: 4g
Saturated Fat: 1g
Cholesterol: 0mg
Sodium: 360mg
Carbohydrates: 24g
Dietary Fiber: 5g
Protein: 7g

1. Bring broth, half-n-half, and butter or margarine to boil, then simmer in medium saucepan over medium heat.
2. Whisk in amaranth. Reduce heat to low, cover, and cook for 25 minutes. Remove lid. Cook additional 10 minutes, stirring occasionally, or until desired consistency. Remove from heat; let sit 5 minutes.
3. Add salt and pepper to taste. If using, stir in chives. Serve while hot.

Alternate Grains: Cornmeal is traditionally used to prepare grits and you can use it here. If you usually add cheese to your grits, choose low-fat or non-fat shredded cheddar for the best taste.

Buckwheat Blueberry Pancakes

Makes 6 pancakes. Serves 3.

The sweetness from the blueberries is a perfect complement to the nuttiness from the buckwheat flour. Enjoy these pancakes during the summer when fresh blueberries are at their peak—or all year round with frozen berries, for lots of antioxidants and fiber.

¼ cup + 1 tablespoon buckwheat flour

¼ cup unbleached all-purpose flour

1 teaspoon double-acting baking powder

1 tablespoon cold, unsalted butter, cut into pieces

1 tablespoon acacia or orange blossom honey

1 large egg

⅓ cup vanilla soy milk

¾ cup fresh, or frozen and thawed, blueberries
   (can also used diced green apples instead)

2 tablespoons maple syrup, warm (optional)

Nutrition Analysis (2 pancakes)

Calories: 190
Calories From Fat: 60
Total Fat: 6g
Saturated Fat: 3g
Cholesterol: 80mg
Sodium: 220mg
Carbohydrates: 28g
Dietary Fiber: 3g
Protein: 6g

1. In medium bowl, combine ¼ cup buckwheat flour, all-purpose flour, baking powder, butter, and honey into a fine crumbled mixture with pastry blender or potato masher.
2. In large bowl, whisk egg and soy milk. Add flour mixture to egg-soy milk mixture. Whisk until batter is well combined. Let stand for 5 minutes. Toss blueberries with 1 tablespoon buckwheat flour. Stir into batter.
3. Preheat oven to 200°F (100°C). Coat large, flat, nonstick skillet or griddle with cooking spray. Place over medium heat.
4. Spoon batter, about 3 tablespoons per pancake, onto hot surface. Cook pancakes in batches, 2 minutes per side, or until cooked through. Transfer cooked pancakes to a heatproof platter and keep warm in oven. Serve with maple syrup.

Alternate Grains: For a darker, earthier pancake, use ½ cup buckwheat flour instead of ¼ cup buckwheat plus ¼ cup all-purpose flour.

Buckwheat Crepes with Ham and Cheese

Makes 6 crepes. Serves 6.

*T here's nothing quite like the taste of freshly prepared crepes.
Consider it Parisian pleasure on a plate, one that is high in
protein and a good source of calcium, selenium, and zinc.*

1 large egg

⅔ cup cold 1% or fat-free milk

1 tablespoon unsalted butter or trans-free
   margarine, melted

¼ cup buckwheat flour

¼ cup unbleached all-purpose flour

1 tablespoon canola oil

1 tablespoon Dijon mustard, or to taste

6 slices natural, lean, baked ham or turkey
   ham, halved

1 cup shredded Gruyere or other Swiss cheese

½ teaspoon freshly ground black pepper, or to taste

**Nutrition Analysis
(1 crepe)**

Calories: 200
Calories From Fat: 110
Total Fat: 12g
Saturated Fat: 4.5g
Cholesterol: 75mg
Sodium: 410mg
Carbohydrates: 8g
Dietary Fiber: 1g
Protein: 14g

1. Blend egg, milk, butter, and flours at high speed for 1 minute, or
   until no lumps remain. Refrigerate, covered, for at least 1 hour.
2. Add ½ teaspoon oil to nonstick crepe pan or nonstick sauté pan
   over medium heat. Spoon about 3 tablespoons batter into pan,
   tilting pan to coat. Cook 1 minute or until edges begin to pull away
   from the pan and bottom is lightly browned. Flip crepe over and
   cook 30 seconds, or until lightly browned. Repeat with remaining
   oil and batter to make 6 crepes. Preheat oven to 350°F (180°C).
3. Atop each crepe, brush Dijon mustard, add 2 halves ham slices, and
   sprinkle cheese and pepper. Fold edges over, place on large tray,
   heat in oven for 5 minutes, or until cheese is melted. Serve warm.

Alternate Grains: For a darker, earthier crepe, see left. For fusion
flair, use whole-wheat tortillas: fill each tortilla, then brush tortillas with oil; cook in oven or in skillet until cheese melts.

Southwestern Corn and Red Potato Hash Browns

Makes about 4 cups. Serves 4.

You'll love getting your veggies in the morning with this southwestern side. Much healthier than traditional hash browns, with a lot less fat and more fiber, vitamins C, B$_6$, and K, and potassium from the corn and parsley.

1½ tablespoons extra-virgin olive oil

1 small or ½ large red onion, finely chopped

1 small jalapeno pepper (remove half or all the seeds), minced

2 large boiled red potatoes with skin, chilled, diced

¾ cup frozen and thawed, or canned, yellow corn, drained

½ teaspoon garlic salt, or to taste

¼ cup chopped fresh Italian parsley

**Nutrition Analysis
(1 cup)**

Calories: 210
Calories From Fat: 50
Total Fat: 6g
Saturated Fat: 1g
Cholesterol: 0mg
Sodium: 135mg
Carbohydrates: 36g
Dietary Fiber: 4g
Protein: 4g

1. Add oil to large nonstick skillet over medium-high heat. Once oil is hot, add onion and jalapeno; sauté for 5 minutes, or until lightly browned.
2. Add potatoes and corn. Cook for 5 minutes or until potatoes are lightly browned, stirring potato mixture occasionally.
3. Add garlic salt to taste. Sprinkle with parsley.

Alternate Grains: Experiment with various types of corn. And when corn is in season, use fresh boiled corn in this recipe.

Whole-Grain Corn Huevos Rancheros with Tomatillo Salsa

Makes 4 topped tortillas. Serves 4.

What's one of the most mouthwatering ways to eat corn? Corn tortillas, of course. So, go ahead, kickstart the day by saying "hola tortillas." It's a good source of protein and will satisfy you for hours.

4 6-inch (15 cm) diameter whole grain corn tortillas

1 teaspoon corn or extra-virgin olive oil

2 large eggs

3 large egg whites

¼ teaspoon freshly ground black pepper, or to taste

½ cup shredded reduced-fat Monterey Jack cheese

½ California avocado, peeled, diced

½ cup jarred tomatillo sauce (salsa verde) or tomato-based salsa

2 tablespoons chopped fresh cilantro

Nutrition Analysis (1 tortilla)
Calories: 230
Calories From Fat: 100
Total Fat: 11g
Saturated Fat: 3.5g
Cholesterol: 115mg
Sodium: 380mg
Carbohydrates: 26g
Dietary Fiber: 4g
Protein: 14g

1. For crisp tortillas, coat top and bottom of each tortilla with cooking spray. Place on large baking sheet and bake in 450°F (230°C) oven for 8 minutes (4 minutes per side), or until crisp and lightly browned. Alternatively, for soft tortillas, warm them according to package directions.
2. Meanwhile, place nonstick skillet over medium heat. In a bowl, whisk eggs, egg whites, and pepper. Add oil to skillet. Once hot, pour eggs into skillet. Scramble until fully cooked.
3. Place one portion of eggs atop each tortilla. Immediately, top each with cheese, avocado, sauce/salsa, and cilantro.

Alternate Grains: Use yellow or white corn tortillas, or try whole-wheat or sprouted-grain tortillas, too. Both are delicious for this meal, as well as for sandwiches and quesadillas.

Oat-Bran Banana Walnut Muffins

Makes 12 muffins. Serves 12.

*T*hese perfectly portioned muffins are light on fat, but heavy on flavor. The vitamins and minerals from the oats will give you energy, and the fiber will keep your stomach feeling full and satisfied.

¼ cup corn or canola oil

1 cup granulated sugar

2 large eggs, well beaten

1 cup old-fashioned rolled oats

1 cup unbleached all-purpose flour

¼ cup oat bran

1 teaspoon baking soda

¼ teaspoon fine sea salt

3 large fully ripened bananas, peeled and mashed

2 teaspoons pure vanilla extract

¼ cup chopped walnuts

Nutrition Analysis (1 muffin)

Calories: 220
Calories From Fat: 70
Total Fat: 8g
Saturated Fat: 1g
Cholesterol: 35mg
Sodium: 170mg
Carbohydrates: 36g
Dietary Fiber: 2g
Protein: 4g

1. Preheat oven to 350°F (180°C). In large mixing bowl, blend oil and sugar. Add beaten eggs; blend well.
2. In a separate bowl, mix together oats, flour, oat bran, baking soda, and salt; add dry ingredients to egg mixture. Mix with large spoon until combined. Add bananas and vanilla. Stir until just combined.
3. Lightly coat cups of nonstick muffin tin with cooking spray. Divide batter evenly among cups, about ¼ cup each. Batter will fill 12 cups. Press walnuts atop muffins.
4. Bake in middle of oven for 25 minutes, or until tops are golden and tester comes out clean. Cool muffins in pan on rack for 10 minutes. Remove muffins from cups and cool on rack.

Alternate Grains: Instead of 1 cup unbleached all-purpose flour, use ⅔ cup unbleached all-purpose flour plus ¼ cup whole-wheat flour. Also, in place of oat bran, try cornmeal.

Yogurt Parfait with Cinnamon-Oat Granola

Makes 4 parfaits. Serves 4.

*T*ake delight in this parfait at breakfast-time—or any time. It's a balanced meal all in one that's bursting with wholesomeness from the protein, calcium, magnesium, iron, and zinc.

1 cup old-fashioned rolled oats

¼ cup slivered almonds

2 tablespoons wheat germ

2 tablespoons shelled sunflower seeds, unsalted

1½ teaspoons ground cinnamon

3 tablespoons acacia or orange blossom honey

2 cups fresh, or frozen and thawed, diced peaches

2 cups non-fat and sugar-free peach or French vanilla yogurt

Nutrition Analysis (1 parfait)

Calories: 280
Calories From Fat: 60
Total Fat: 7g
Saturated Fat: 0.5g
Cholesterol: 0mg
Sodium: 65mg
Carbohydrates: 47g
Dietary Fiber: 5g
Protein: 10g

1. Preheat oven to 325°F (160°C).
2. Thoroughly mix oats, almonds, wheat germ, sunflower seeds, and cinnamon in a medium bowl. Continue to stir while drizzling honey into the mixture until well combined.
3. Spread granola mixture evenly onto nonstick 9x13-inch (22x32 cm) baking pan. Bake for 25 minutes, or until golden brown, stirring occasionally during baking. Remove from oven and let cool slightly before preparing parfaits. (Makes 2¼ cups granola)
4. For serving, layer about ½ cup each granola, yogurt, and peaches into each of four parfait or wine glasses. Experiment with various fruits and yogurts, if desired.

Alternate Grains: Go with an extra ¼ cup oats—that's 1¼ cup total—if you don't want to use the wheat germ. Instead of peaches, use fresh or frozen strawberries, raspberries, or blueberries.

Whole-Grain French Toast with Mango-Kiwi Salsa

Makes 8 toasts. Serves 4.

P *erhaps a better name for this entrée is Tropical Toast. The mango and kiwi provides 100% of your vitamin C requirements for one day. It's also packed with fiber, B vitamins, selenium, and manganese.*

2 large eggs

4 large egg whites

⅓ cup vanilla soy milk

⅓ cup apricot or mango nectar

8 slices whole-grain, low-calorie bread

4 teaspoons unsalted butter or trans-free margarine

1 medium mango, peeled, diced

2 medium kiwis, peeled, diced

1 tablespoon pure maple syrup, or to taste

Nutrition Analysis (2 slices)
Calories: 270
Calories From Fat: 70
Total Fat: 8g
Saturated Fat: 1.5g
Cholesterol: 110mg
Sodium: 340mg
Carbohydrates: 42g
Dietary Fiber: 7g
Protein: 12g

1. In medium bowl, whisk eggs, egg whites, soy milk, and nectar. Arrange bread in two 9x13-inch (22x32 cm) baking pans. Evenly distribute egg mixture over bread, flipping slices over to coat both sides. Cover with plastic and refrigerate at least 30 minutes or overnight.
2. Meanwhile, gently stir the mango, kiwi, and maple syrup in small bowl for the salsa; set aside.
3. Melt 1 teaspoon butter in large, flat, nonstick skillet over medium heat. Add bread to skillet in batches and cook 2 minutes per side, or until golden brown, adding more butter to pan as necessary.
4. Transfer to platter. Top each with about 3 tablespoons salsa when serving. Drizzle with additional maple syrup, if desired.

Alternate Grains: Try with various types of whole-grain breads, including whole-wheat and oatmeal bread. To reduce calories, use sugar-free or "lite" maple syrup, and use nonstick butter flavor spray instead of margarine in the pan.

Soups & Salads

Barley and Mushroom Soup with Zucchini

Makes 7 ¼ cups. Serves 6.

This pleasantly filling, pearled barley-packed soup is best during the summertime when zucchinis are in season. It's also loaded with plenty of fiber, vitamins C and K, selenium, potassium, and manganese.

2 tablespoons extra-virgin olive oil
1 large white onion, sliced
2 large cloves garlic, minced
8 cups reduced-sodium beef broth
1 bay leaf
1 cup pearled barley
2½ cups fresh baby bella mushrooms, thinly sliced
1 medium zucchini, halved lengthwise, thinly sliced crosswise
1 teaspoon chopped fresh thyme
2 tablespoons chopped fresh parsley

Nutrition Analysis
(1¼ cups)
Calories: 230
Calories From Fat: 60
Total Fat: 7g
Saturated Fat: 1.5g
Cholesterol: 0mg
Sodium: 105mg
Carbohydrates: 32g
Dietary Fiber: 6g
Protein: 11g

1. Add oil to stockpot over medium heat. Once oil is hot, add onion; sauté for 5 minutes. Add garlic; sauté for 1 minute.
2. Add broth, 2 cups water, bay leaf, and barley; bring to boil over high heat. Reduce heat to medium; cover and cook for 50 minutes, or until barley is nearly tender. Remove bay leaf.
3. Add mushrooms, zucchini, and thyme; cook covered for 8 minutes, or until vegetables and barley are tender. If necessary, add more broth to desired consistency.
4. Ladle soup into bowls. Sprinkle with parsley.

Alternate Grains: Try this soup with the whole-grain hull-less barley. However, note it will take significantly longer to cook — about 1½ hours. Additional broth will likely be needed.

Hearty Millet and Butternut Squash Soup

Makes 8 cups. Serves 8.

C*all it irony in a cup. Millet is considered one of the oldest grains in the world. Yet, this soup with its brilliant orange color and intriguing creamy yet millet-studded texture is 100% modern. And with 400% of your daily requirement for vitamin A, and 70% of your vitamin C needs, this squash soup will surely keep you healthy.*

5½ cups reduced-sodium chicken or vegetable
   broth
¾ cup hulled millet
1 medium butternut squash, peeled, seeds
   removed, cut into cubes
1 cup low-fat plain soy milk
¼ teaspoon hot pepper sauce, or to taste
3 tablespoons finely chopped fresh chives

**Nutrition Analysis
(1 cup)**
Calories: 180
Calories From Fat: 10
Total Fat: 1g
Saturated Fat: 0g
Cholesterol: 0mg
Sodium: 410mg
Carbohydrates: 39g
Dietary Fiber: 6g
Protein: 7g

1. In large stockpot, bring broth to boil over high
heat. Add millet and simmer, covered, over medium-low heat
for 30 minutes, or until millet is well cooked.
2. Add squash and soy milk; stir. Simmer, covered, another 30
minutes, or until squash is fork-tender.
3. Puree mixture in pot using an immersion blender. Alternatively,
puree slightly cooled soup mixture in batches in standing electric
blender until creamy. Pour pureed soup into clean stockpot.
4. If necessary, add more broth to desired consistency. To the
simmering soup, add hot pepper sauce and salt to taste. Stir in
or top with chives.

Alternate Grains: This soup will be lovely with amaranth in place of
millet—and creamier, too.

Amaranth Chicken Salad with Tarragon and Almonds

Makes 4 cups. Serves 4.

*A*maranth provides a caviarlike texture to make this chicken salad *like no other. Using low-fat ingredients, this salad is high in protein and a rich source of niacin, vitamin B$_6$, selenium, and magnesium.*

⅓ cup amaranth

12 oz (340 g) poached or roasted boneless, skinless chicken breast, cut into cubes, chilled

1 stalk celery, thinly sliced

¼ cup minced Vidalia onion

⅓ cup fat-free sour cream

2 tablespoons lite mayonnaise

2 tablespoons fat-free plain yogurt

1 tablespoon apple cider vinegar

1 tablespoon chopped fresh tarragon, or to taste

Pinch of salt (optional)

4 large Boston or other lettuce leaves

¼ cup sliced almonds, pan-toasted

Nutrition Analysis (1 cup)
Calories: 240
Calories From Fat: 80
Total Fat: 8g
Saturated Fat: 1.5g
Cholesterol: 45mg
Sodium: 150mg
Carbohydrates: 19g
Dietary Fiber: 4g
Protein: 22g

1. In small saucepan over medium-high heat bring amaranth and 1 cup water to boil; reduce heat to medium-low and cover. Simmer for 15 minutes, or until tender. Remove from heat. Let sit for 5 minutes covered. Transfer to bowl. Chill.
2. In another bowl, combine chicken, celery, and onion.
3. Mix sour cream, mayonnaise, yogurt, vinegar, and tarragon into amaranth. Combine with chicken mixture. Refrigerate at least 30 minutes before serving to allow flavors to combine. Add salt to taste.
4. Serve 1 cup of amaranth chicken salad on each lettuce leaf. Sprinkle with almonds.

Alternate Grains: Quinoa, millet, or whole-wheat couscous is the best alternative to amaranth in this salad.

Barley, Corn, and Arugula Salad with Goat Cheese

Makes 12 cups. Serves 6.

Corn is at its seasonal best from June to September, so make sure to add this flavorful recipe to that Memorial, Independence, or Labor Day cookout. And for a real treat, try it with grilled corn on the cob.

½ cup pearled barley

2 bunches arugula, coarsely chopped

1 cup fresh corn (cooked, chilled, and cut from cob) or frozen and thawed, corn kernels

¼ cup chopped fresh chives

2 tablespoons extra-virgin olive oil

3 tablespoons apple cider vinegar

3 tablespoons minced shallots

2 teaspoons Dijon mustard

¼ teaspoon fine sea salt, or to taste

¼ teaspoon freshly ground black pepper, or to taste

⅓ cup soft reduced-fat goat cheese, crumbled, plus 1 tablespoon crumbled

Nutrition Analysis (2 cups)
Calories: 170
Calories From Fat: 60
Total Fat: 7g
Saturated Fat: 2g
Cholesterol: 0mg
Sodium: 110mg
Carbohydrates: 23g
Dietary Fiber: 5g
Protein: 5g

1. In medium saucepan over high heat bring barley and 2¼ cups water to boil; reduce heat to medium-low and cover. Simmer for 45 minutes, or until chewy yet tender. Remove from heat. Let sit for 10 minutes covered. Transfer to bowl. Chill. (Note: This step can be done in advance.)
2. In large bowl, mix chilled barley with arugula, corn, and chives.
3. Whisk oil, vinegar, shallots, and mustard in small bowl. Pour dressing over barley mixture to coat.
4. Add salt and pepper to taste. Sprinkle with goat cheese.

Alternate Grains: Spelt or triticale berries would provide a similar bite to this salad.

161

Buckwheat Noodle, Artichoke, and Tofu Salad

Makes about 6 cups. Serves 6.

T*his zingy soba noodle salad has it all—flavor appeal, eye appeal, and nutritional appeal with protein and minerals. Plus, the pine nuts provide texture and taste great.*

⅓ cup rice vinegar

2 tablespoons minced shallots

8 oz (225 g) dry buckwheat soba noodles

1½ tablespoons extra-virgin olive oil

1 cup thinly sliced, frozen and thawed, or canned, water-packed artichoke hearts, drained

½ of 14-oz (400 g) package (drained weight), extra-firm tofu, drained, cut into cubes (about 1 cup)

⅓ cup finely sliced or chopped fresh basil, plus additional for garnish

⅛ teaspoon fine sea salt, or to taste

3 tablespoons pine nuts, toasted

Nutrition Analysis (1 cup)
Calories: 240
Calories From Fat: 80
Total Fat: 9g
Saturated Fat: 1g
Cholesterol: 0mg
Sodium: 540mg
Carbohydrates: 33g
Dietary Fiber: 2g
Protein: 11g

1. In small bowl, whisk vinegar and shallots; set aside.
2. Cook noodles in boiling water until al dente—approximately 1 minute less than suggested by package directions. Drain. Toss noodles in large bowl with 1 tablespoon oil. Toss with vinegar-shallot mixture and artichoke hearts. Chill.
3. Meanwhile, in nonstick skillet over medium heat, add remaining oil. Once oil is hot, add tofu cubes. Sauté for 10 minutes, or until golden brown on all sides. Remove from pan.
4. Toss noodles with tofu cubes, basil, and pine nuts. Add salt to taste. Serve chilled or at room temperature. Garnish with additional basil.

Alternate Grains: Enjoy with various types of pasta: whole-wheat linguine, udon noodles, or whole-wheat orzo.

Lemon Bulgur Salad with Chickpeas, Roasted Peppers, and Light Jalapeno Dressing

Makes 6 cups. Serves 8.

This bulgur salad is a bit mixed up—part Middle Eastern, part Italian, part Mexican—but all of your taste buds will be mesmerized by the worldly mix. With lots of fiber and vitamin C, it will surely fill you up and keep you healthy.

1½ cups medium grain (#2) bulgur

½ cup fresh lemon juice

1 large clove garlic, minced

1 can (15 oz, 425 g) unsalted, canned chickpeas, rinsed and drained

½ of 16-oz (450 g) jar roasted red peppers, drained, diced (¾ cup diced)

¼ cup chopped fresh Italian parsley leaves

2 tablespoons extra-virgin olive oil

2 tablespoons reduced-sodium vegetable or chicken broth

1 jalapeno pepper (with seeds), minced

¼ teaspoon fine sea salt, or to taste

Nutrition Analysis (¾ cup)

Calories: 210
Calories From Fat: 40
Total Fat: 4.5g
Saturated Fat: 0.5g
Cholesterol: 0mg
Sodium: 370mg
Carbohydrates: 34g
Dietary Fiber: 7g
Protein: 7g

1. Place bulgur in large bowl. Add 3 cups boiling water and set aside for 20 minutes. Drain bulgur well in strainer, gently pressing out excess liquid.
2. Return bulgur to bowl and stir in ¼ cup lemon juice and garlic. Stir in chickpeas, roasted peppers, and parsley.
3. Whisk remaining lemon juice, oil, broth, jalapeno, and salt in small bowl. Drizzle jalapeno dressing over the bulgur mixture and toss to combine.

Alternate Grains: Use quinoa for a nice change of taste and texture for this salad.

Toasted Corn and Bulgur Salad with Grape Tomatoes

Makes 4 cups. Serves 4.

This salad is highly nutritious because of the vitamins A, C, and K as well as magnesium and fiber. Toasting the bulgur in this salad adds nuttiness. Toasting the corn—also considered caramelizing—adds sweetness, naturally.

¾ cup medium-grain (#2) bulgur
1 cup tomato juice
1 tablespoon extra-virgin olive oil
¾ cup fresh corn (cooked, chilled, and cut from cob) or frozen and thawed corn kernels
1 cup grape tomatoes, ½ very thinly sliced horizontally, ½ halved or quartered lengthwise
¼ cup chopped fresh chives
¼ cup chopped or thinly sliced fresh basil
2 tablespoons aged red wine vinegar, or to taste
1 teaspoon freshly ground black pepper, or to taste

Nutrition Analysis (1 cup)
Calories: 160
Calories From Fat: 35
Total Fat: 4g
Saturated Fat: 0.5g
Cholesterol: 0mg
Sodium: 170mg
Carbohydrates: 29g
Dietary Fiber: 6g
Protein: 5g

1. In large skillet, toast bulgur over medium heat for 6 minutes, or until lightly browned, stirring occasionally.
2. Add tomato juice and ½ cup water; bring to boil. Reduce heat and simmer covered for 5 minutes. Remove from heat, keep covered, and let stand 10 minutes. Transfer to bowl and chill.
3. Add oil to skillet over medium-high heat. Once oil is hot, sauté corn for 2 minutes, or until golden brown. Chill.
4. Gently stir corn, very thinly sliced tomatoes, chives, basil, and vinegar into bulgur. Add pepper to taste. Serve with halved or quartered tomatoes arranged atop the salad.

Alternate Grains: Whole-wheat orzo or couscous would work nicely in this salad. Or make corn the star. Skip the bulgur and tomato juice, use 2 cups corn, and keep everything else the same.

Quinoa and Fresh Baby Spinach, Feta, and Toasted Pine Nut Salad

Makes 6 cups. Serves 6.

If quinoa is the world's healthiest grain, then this might be the world's healthiest salad since it's jam-packed with so many vitamins and minerals. What's more, this might be one of the easiest and tastiest, too.

1 cup quinoa

Juice of 1 lemon (about 3 tablespoons)

3 tablespoons extra-virgin olive oil

⅛ teaspoon fine sea salt, or to taste

2 cups fresh baby spinach

⅓ cup crumbled feta cheese

½ cup finely sliced scallions (about 3)

½ cup grape tomatoes, halved, or cherry
  tomatoes, quartered

3 tablespoons finely chopped fresh mint or
  basil (or mixture)

3 tablespoons pine nuts, pan-toasted

**Nutrition Analysis
(1 cup)**
Calories: 230
Calories From Fat: 120
Total Fat: 13g
Saturated Fat: 3g
Cholesterol: 5mg
Sodium: 160mg
Carbohydrates: 23g
Dietary Fiber: 3g
Protein: 6g

1. In medium saucepan over high heat bring quinoa and 2 cups water to boil; reduce heat to medium and cover. Cook for 12 minutes, or until tender. Remove from heat. Let sit for 5 minutes covered.
2. Meanwhile, whisk lemon juice, oil, and salt in large bowl. Add hot quinoa to dressing and stir with fork. Chill.
3. Toss the chilled quinoa with spinach, feta, scallions, tomatoes, and herbs.
4. Top with pine nuts and serve.

Alternate Grains: Whole-wheat couscous or orzo is ideal in place of quinoa in this recipe.

Grecian Spelt, Cucumber, Dill, and Mint Salad

Makes 3¼ cups. Serves 4.

Traditional tabbouleh salad gets an extreme Greek makeover here. This wheat-free, tomato-free twist uses spelt instead of bulgur, which adds a mild hazelnut-like taste and extra protein, and vitamins C and K.

½ cup spelt

¼ cup fresh lemon juice

2 tablespoons extra-virgin olive oil

1 large clove garlic, minced

½ of 14-inch (35 cm) hothouse cucumber, diced

½ cup chopped scallions, chopped (about 3)

¼ cup chopped fresh dill

¼ cup chopped fresh mint

½ teaspoon freshly ground black pepper, or to taste

¼ teaspoon fine sea salt, or to taste

¼ cup crumbled feta cheese

Nutrition Analysis (¾ cup)
Calories: 180
Calories From Fat: 90
Total Fat: 10g
Saturated Fat: 2.5g
Cholesterol: 10mg
Sodium: 250mg
Carbohydrates: 21g
Dietary Fiber: 1g
Protein: 5g

1. In small saucepan over high heat bring spelt and 2¾ cups water to boil; reduce heat to medium-low and cover. Simmer for 1 hour 15 minutes, or until chewy, yet tender. Remove from heat. Let sit for 10 minutes covered. Transfer to bowl. Chill. (Note: This step can be done in advance.)
2. Meanwhile, whisk lemon juice, oil, and garlic in medium bowl to blend. Add chilled spelt. Stir with fork.
3. Stir in cucumber, scallions, dill, and mint. Add pepper and salt to taste. Toss, top with feta cheese, and serve.

Alternate Grains: Make this salad more like traditional tabbouleh by using bulgur. Try triticale for a bigger bite, or even brown rice.

Triticale Berries and Roasted Asian Eggplant Salad with Peanuts

Makes 4 cups. Serves 4.

ew people are familiar with triticale, yet it is an excellent source of fiber and contains lots of vitamins and minerals. So, discover its uniqueness in this salad filled with Asian goodness.

⅓ cup triticale berries

4 Asian eggplants

Juice of 1½ limes (about 3 tablespoons)

3 tablespoons thinly sliced shallots

2 scallions, thinly sliced (green and white parts)

2 tablespoons chopped fresh cilantro

1 tablespoon Asian garlic-chili sauce

1 tablespoon acacia or orange blossom honey

2 teaspoons natural, low-sodium soy sauce

2 tablespoons chopped, unsalted, roasted nuts

Nutrition Analysis (1 cup)

Calories: 140
Calories From Fat: 25
Total Fat: 3g
Saturated Fat: 0g
Cholesterol: 0mg
Sodium: 210mg
Carbohydrates: 27g
Dietary Fiber: 7g
Protein: 5g

1. In small saucepan over high heat, bring triticale and 2 cups water to boil; reduce heat to medium-low and cover. Simmer for 1 hour, or until chewy yet tender. Remove from heat. Let sit for 10 minutes covered. Transfer to bowl. Chill.

2. Wrap each eggplant in foil. Roast in 400°F (200°C) oven for 20 minutes, or until cooked through. Chill.

3. Meanwhile, place lime juice, shallots, scallions, cilantro, garlic-chili sauce, honey, and soy sauce in medium bowl. Stir to combine. Cut off the stem of each chilled eggplant. Slice each eggplant in half lengthwise; cut each half into 2 or 3 slices lengthwise, then into small bite-size pieces crosswise. Toss eggplant pieces and triticale with the mixture in the medium bowl till coated.

4. Before serving, top with peanuts and garnish with cilantro sprigs.

Alternate Grains: Spelt is hearty enough to be showcased like triticale in this Asian-inspired salad.

Appetizers
& Snacks

Amaranth-Zucchini Squash Patties

Makes 14 patties. Serves 7.

Do you like potato pancakes? Then you'll love these amaranth patties. A perfect party food, with only 100 calories for 2 patties and lots of vitamins and minerals, they are quite nutritious.

½ cup amaranth

½ cup grated zucchini squash, well drained
    (about ½ medium zucchini)

¼ cup minced Vidalia onion

¼ cup amaranth flour

1 large egg

¾ teaspoon garlic salt

¼ teaspoon hot pepper sauce, or to taste

¼ cup fat-free sour cream (optional)

**Nutrition Analysis
(2 squash patties)**
Calories: 100
Calories From Fat: 15
Total Fat: 2g
Saturated Fat: 0.5g
Cholesterol: 30mg
Sodium: 110mg
Carbohydrates: 15g
Dietary Fiber: 3g
Protein: 5g

1. In small saucepan (preferably nonstick) over high heat, bring amaranth and 1½ cups water to boil. Reduce heat to medium-low and cover. Simmer for 20 minutes, or until grains are softened and water is nearly absorbed. Remove from heat and let sit, covered, for 5 minutes.

2. Meanwhile, in medium bowl, mix zucchini, onion, flour, egg, garlic salt, and hot pepper sauce. Stir in hot cooked amaranth until well combined. (Note: Makes 1¾ cups batter.)

3. Place large nonstick pan or griddle over medium heat. Once hot, drop amaranth-zucchini mixture by spoon onto pan, about 2 table-spoons per patty, flattening with back of spoon to form round patties. Cook 4 to 5 minutes per side, or until golden brown, only turning after completely done on first side. Serve each topped with about a teaspoon dollop of fat-free sour cream, if desired.

Alternate Grains: Other whole grain flours will work fine in place of the amaranth flour.

Buckwheat Crepes with Goat Cheese and Sun-Dried Tomatoes

Makes 8 small crepes. Serves 4.

C repes, often enjoyed in the morning, make a popular late-day light bite or appetizer when filled with high-flavored ingredients, like goat cheese and sun-dried tomatoes. It's a virtual taste explosion.

⅔ cup cold 1% or fat-free milk

1 large egg

1 tablespoon unsalted butter or trans-free margarine, melted

¼ cup buckwheat flour

¼ cup unbleached all-purpose flour

½ cup soft, low-fat goat cheese

5 sun-dried tomato halves (not oil-packed), finely chopped

¼ teaspoon garlic powder, or to taste

4 teaspoons extra-virgin olive oil

**Nutrition Analysis
(2 crepes)**

Calories: 210
Calories From Fat: 120
Total Fat: 13g
Saturated Fat: 4g
Cholesterol: 60mg
Sodium: 310mg
Carbohydrates: 16g
Dietary Fiber: 2g
Protein: 8g

1. Blend milk, egg, butter, and flours at high speed for 45 seconds, or until batter is smooth. Cover and refrigerate for at least 1 hour.
2. Meanwhile, in small bowl stir goat cheese, sun-dried tomatoes, and garlic powder until well combined; chill until ready to use.
3. Preheat oven to 350°F (180°C). Add ½ teaspoon oil to crepe pan over medium heat. Spoon about 2 tablespoons batter into pan, tilting pan to make thin circular crepe. Cook 1 minute or until edges begin to pull away from the pan and bottom is lightly browned. Flip crepe over and cook 30 seconds, or until lightly browned. Repeat with remaining oil and batter to make 8 crepes.
4. Atop each crepe, spread cheese mixture. Fold edges over, place on large tray, and heat in oven for 5 minutes. Serve warm.

Alternate Grains: For a darker, earthier crepe, use ½ cup buckwheat flour instead of ¼ cup buckwheat plus ¼ cup all-purpose flour.

Herbed Bulgur-Stuffed Tomatoes with Toasted Pine Nuts

Makes 4 cups. Serves 4.

Bulgur is a Middle Eastern mainstay. Packed with 12 grams of fiber and 60% of your vitamin C and A requirement in one serving, as well as iron, potassium, zinc, and magnesium, this dish is super healthy.

4 large tomatoes
2 tablespoons extra-virgin olive oil
1 large red onion, finely chopped
1 cup medium (#2) or coarse-grain bulgur
½ cup fresh baby spinach leaves
¼ teaspoon fine sea salt, or to taste
¼ teaspoon freshly ground black pepper
⅓ cup pine nuts, pan-toasted
⅓ cup chopped fresh parsley
3 tablespoons chopped fresh mint
2 tablespoons lemon juice or aged red wine vinegar

**Nutrition Analysis
(1 stuffed tomato)**
Calories: 330
Calories From Fat: 150
Total Fat: 16g
Saturated Fat: 2g
Cholesterol: 0mg
Sodium: 220mg
Carbohydrates: 43g
Dietary Fiber: 12g
Protein: 9g

1. Cut off top third of tomatoes. Remove seeds and core from top portions; dice and set aside. Scoop out insides of the large tomatoes to create tomato "shells." Sit tomato "shells" cut-side down on paper towels to drain.
2. Heat oil in large saucepan over medium heat. Once hot, cook onion in oil, stirring occasionally, for 8 minutes or until softened and lightly browned. Add bulgur, spinach, salt, and pepper, and cook, stirring for 1 minute or until spinach is wilted.
3. Add 1 cup water, then remove from heat and let stand, covered, for 30 minutes or until bulgur is softened.
4. Stir in pine nuts, parsley, mint, and lemon juice or vinegar. Mound bulgur filling into tomato "shells." Sprinkle with diced tomato. Serve at room temperature. Enjoy with a knife and fork.

Alternate Grains: Quinoa or whole-wheat couscous will be an ideal replacement for bulgur here.

Cornmeal-Crusted Oven-Fried Chicken Fingers

Makes 12 fingers. Serves 6.

A fun finger food, for sure, and a crunchy kid pleaser, too. With a lot less fat than traditional fried chicken, this recipe gives all the taste without the guilt. Perfect for parties or as an entree.

½ cup unbleached all-purpose flour

1 large egg

1 large egg white

½ teaspoon freshly ground black pepper

¼ teaspoon cayenne pepper

¾ cup very fine whole-grain cornmeal

½ teaspoon garlic powder

1 pound (450 g) boneless, skinless chicken
    breasts, sliced diagonally into 12 long strips
    (fingers)

6 tablespoons honey mustard or salsa of choice

**Nutrition Analysis
(2 chicken fingers)**
Calories: 250
Calories From Fat: 20
Total Fat: 2g
Saturated Fat: 0.5g
Cholesterol: 80mg
Sodium: 230mg
Carbohydrates: 33g
Dietary Fiber: 2g
Protein: 23g

1. Preheat oven to 375°F (190°C). In shallow bowl add flour. In second shallow bowl whisk egg and egg whites with 2 tablespoons cold water and the peppers. In third shallow bowl combine cornmeal with ½ teaspoon garlic powder.
2. Season chicken "fingers" with remaining garlic powder. Dip the chicken into flour, then egg mixture, and then cornmeal mixture.
3. Lightly coat each piece of chicken with butter-flavor cooking spray while placing into 9x13-inch (22x32 cm) nonstick baking pan.
4. Bake for 20-22 minutes, until internal chicken temperature reaches 170°F (76°C), turning over after 12 minutes. Serve hot or at room temperature with honey mustard or salsa of choice.

Alternate Grains: These "fingers" will be nice and crispy when using whole-wheat breadcrumbs instead of cornmeal. Lightly crunched whole-grain corn flakes cereal will make these even crispier.

Oatcakes with Goat Cheese and Dried Plum

Makes 16. Serves 8.

*O*atcakes *are a traditional favorite of Scotland. Here, homemade oat-cakes take on a nontraditional, fancy flair. Served as an appetizer or as a lunch entrée over field greens, they will surely satisfy any appetite.*

1 cup old-fashioned rolled oats

2 tablespoons unbleached flour

½ teaspoon fine sea salt

½ teaspoon baking powder

2 tablespoons cold unsalted butter, cut into bits

2–3 tablespoons 1% milk

½ cup finely sliced dried plums

¼ cup pomegranate or cranberry juice

2 teaspoons finely chopped fresh thyme leaves

⅓ cup soft, tangy low-fat goat cheese

16 fresh tiny thyme sprigs

**Nutrition Analysis
(2 oatcakes)**

Calories: 100
Calories From Fat: 40
Total Fat: 4.5g
Saturated Fat: 2.5g
Cholesterol: 10mg
Sodium: 220mg
Carbohydrates: 14g
Dietary Fiber: 2g
Protein: 2g

1. Preheat oven to 375°F (190°C). In food processor, pulse oats until finely chopped. Add flour, salt, baking powder, and butter, and pulse until mixture resembles coarse meal. Add 2 tablespoons milk and pulse until dough forms (can add 1 more tablespoon milk).
2. On lightly floured surface roll dough into a 6-inch (15 cm) diameter circle. With a 2-inch (5 cm) round cookie-cutter, cut 16 oatcakes; put them on nonstick baking sheets 1 inch (2.5 cm) apart. Bake in middle of oven 12–15 minutes, until crisp. Transfer to rack to cool.
3. In small saucepan, combine plums, juice, and 2 teaspoons thyme; simmer for 5 minutes, stirring occasionally, or until most liquid is evaporated. Transfer plum mixture to a small bowl and cool.
4. Top each oatcake with about ½ tablespoon plum mixture, 1 teaspoon goat cheese, and a thyme sprig.

Alternate Grains: Boost whole grains further by using any whole-grain flour in place of all-purpose flour.

Quinoa Tuna Salad Sandwich on Whole-Wheat Bread

Makes 3 cups tuna salad; ½ cup per sandwich.

A tuna salad sandwich is one of the all-time classics. But you'll find a favorite new variation with this quinoa-accented version. To jazz up the sandwich, add sprouts, avocado, lettuce, and tomato.

½ cup quinoa
⅓ cup plain fat-free yogurt
3 tablespoons soybean or canola mayonnaise
2 tablespoons spicy Dijon mustard
Juice of 1 small or ½ large lemon (about
   2 tablespoons)
1 can (6 oz, 170 g) solid white tuna in spring
   water, drained
1 cup grape tomatoes, sliced or halved
½ cup finely diced Vidalia or other sweet onion
¼ cup chopped fresh Italian parsley
12 slices light whole-wheat bread (toasted, if desired)

Nutrition Analysis (1 sandwich)
Calories: 240
Calories From Fat: 70
Total Fat: 8g
Saturated Fat: 1g
Cholesterol: 15mg
Sodium: 480mg
Carbohydrates: 32g
Dietary Fiber: 8g
Protein: 14g

1. In small saucepan over high heat, bring quinoa and 1 cup water to boil. reduce heat to medium and cover. Simmer for 7 minutes or until quinoa has absorbed the water. Remove from the heat. Let sit for 5 minutes covered. Chill.
2. In large bowl, whisk yogurt, mayonnaise, mustard, and lemon juice until well combined.
3. Stir in tuna and quinoa until coated. Stir in tomatoes, onions, and parsley.
4. Serve on bread. Slice sandwich diagonally.

Alternate Grains: Use amaranth instead of quinoa for a creamier texture. To reduce calories, serve tuna open face on 1 slice of lite bread, or wrapped in lettuce leaves; you can also use lite mayonnaise instead to reduce the calorie count.

Main Courses

Sesame Amaranth and Salmon with Zucchini and Broccoli

Makes 5 cups rice-vegetable mixture. Serves 4.

*J*ust one bite of this appealing entrée will transport you to Asia. This dish is an excellent source of omega 3 fatty acids, folate, vitamins C, B_6, and B_{12}, and provides 70% of your daily requirement of selenium.

2 teaspoons toasted sesame oil

1 cup amaranth

2 large cloves garlic, minced

1½ cups orange juice

4 x 3-oz (85 g) wild salmon filets

2 cups bite-size broccoli florets

1 medium zucchini, halved vertically, then sliced
    horizontally

2 teaspoons light (reduced-sodium) soy sauce

1 teaspoon acacia or orange blossom honey

2 teaspoons toasted sesame seeds

Nutrition Analysis
(1 salmon filet)
Calories: 390
Calories From Fat: 90
Total Fat: 10g
Saturated Fat: 1.5g
Cholesterol: 45mg
Sodium: 340mg
Carbohydrates: 52g
Dietary Fiber: 3g
Protein: 24g

1. Add 1 teaspoon oil to medium saucepan over medium heat. Once oil is hot, add brown rice and cook for 1 minute. Add orange juice, ⅔ cup water, and garlic; bring to boil over high heat. Cover, reduce heat to low. Simmer for 55 minutes, or until rice is tender.
2. Preheat oven to 425°F (220°C). Line a large baking sheet with parchment paper. Place salmon on sheet. Whisk soy sauce and honey in small bowl; drizzle over salmon. Bake salmon uncovered for 8–10 minutes. Remove salmon from oven, cover with foil, and keep warm.
3. Heat remaining oil in a nonstick skillet over medium heat. Sauté vegetables for 2 minutes, then cover and cook on low heat for 5 minutes, or until crisp-tender. Mix vegetables with the cooked rice.
4. Serve on platter topped with salmon. Sprinkle with sesame seeds.

Alternate Grains: Barley or another heartier grains, such as brown rice, will add a nice, chewy texture to this lovely dish.

Italian-Inspired Barley with Escarole and Turkey Sausage

Makes 5 cups. Serves 4.

*I*t takes a while for the barley to cook, but it's all worth it in the end. And for a zippier taste, use a spicy turkey sausage, a much healthier alternative to traditional sausage, with a lot less fat and much more fiber, folate, and vitamins.

1 cup whole hull-less barley

1 tablespoon extra-virgin olive oil

6 oz (170 g) Italian turkey sausage, casings removed

1 head hand-torn escarole

2 large cloves garlic, minced

1 cup reduced-sodium chicken broth

⅓ cup chopped fresh Italian parsley

2 tablespoons freshly grated Parmigiana-Reggiano cheese

Nutrition Analysis (1¼ cups)

Calories: 300
Calories From Fat: 80
Total Fat: 8g
Saturated Fat: 2g
Cholesterol: 35mg
Sodium: 450mg
Carbohydrates: 42g
Dietary Fiber: 10g
Protein: 16g

1. In medium saucepan over high heat, bring barley and 3 cups water to boil; reduce heat to medium-low and cover. Simmer for 45 minutes, or until chewy yet tender.
2. Meanwhile, add oil to large skillet over medium heat. Once oil is hot, add sausage; cook, breaking up clumps, for 5 minutes or until just cooked through; remove sausage, leaving fat in skillet.
3. Add escarole and garlic to skillet; cook, stirring, for 3 minutes, or until greens are wilted.
4. Return sausage, barley, and broth to saucepan. Bring to boil over high heat; remove from heat.
5. Stir in parsley. Add salt to taste. Serve in bowls. Top with cheese.

Alternate Grains: Any small-shaped whole-wheat pasta should work nicely instead of barley. Might be tasty served over whole-wheat couscous, too.

Middle-Eastern Bulgur Meatballs and Caramelized-Onion Tomato Sauce

Makes 18 meatballs. Serves 6.

These meatballs are just like you imagined them. They can either be paired with whole-wheat pasta or are delicious just as is.

1 pound (450 g) lean ground beef or lamb

¾ cup finely chopped fresh parsley, plus additional for garnish, if desired

¼ cup finely chopped fresh mint

½ cup medium-grain (#2) bulgur

4 large cloves garlic, minced

¼ teaspoon fine sea salt, or to taste

½ teaspoon freshly ground black pepper

1 tablespoon extra-virgin olive oil

1 large white onion, thinly sliced

½ cup dry red wine

1 can (1½ cups) organic diced tomatoes with juice

1 cinnamon stick

Nutrition Analysis (3 meatballs)

Calories: 260
Calories From Fat: 90
Total Fat: 10g
Saturated Fat: 3g
Cholesterol: 50mg
Sodium: 330mg
Carbohydrates: 16g
Dietary Fiber: 3g
Protein: 24g

1. In large bowl, combine meat, parsley, mint, bulgur, ½ of the minced garlic, ¼ cup water, and salt and pepper to taste.
2. Shape mixture into 18 meatballs, about 2 tablespoons each. Place on a plate, cover, and chill.
3. Heat oil in large skillet over medium-high heat. Sauté onion for 5 minutes. Add remaining garlic and sauté for 30 seconds. Add wine and cook for 1 minute. Stir in tomatoes and cinnamon stick.
4. Add meatballs to skillet. Add ½ cup water, bring to boil, and reduce the heat to medium-low. Cover and simmer for 20 minutes. Turn meatballs over. Continue cooking uncovered for 10 more minutes or until sauce has thickened. Remove cinnamon stick.

Alternate Grains: Try rolled oats instead of bulgur. They'll turn out to be Mediterranean meatloaf balls.

Kamut Pizza with Spinach and Goat Cheese

Makes 1 (14-inch, 35cm) pizza. Serves 6.

*T*he best part of this pizza is the crust, which has a rich, buttery flavor and lots of fiber. Add other fun, high-fiber toppings to it.

1 packet (¼ oz; 7 g) active dry yeast
4 cups kamut flour, plus extra
    for kneading
1½ tablespoons extra-virgin olive oil
¼ teaspoon fine sea salt
3 cups baby spinach leaves
1 tablespoon fresh lemon juice
4 oz (115 g) soft, low-fat goat cheese, crumbled
2 tablespoons chopped fresh basil
¼ teaspoon freshly ground black pepper
¼ teaspoon garlic powder, or to taste

Nutrition Analysis
(1 slice)
Calories: 330
Calories From Fat: 70
Total Fat: 8g
Saturated Fat: 2g
Cholesterol: 5mg
Sodium: 200mg
Carbohydrates: 53g
Dietary Fiber: 9g
Protein: 12g

1. In medium bowl, combine yeast and 1⅓ cups warm water. Let stand for 10 minutes or until yeast softens. In large bowl, add flour. Make a well in center. Pour yeast mixture into well. Stir vigorously with spoon until smooth. Place dough on lightly floured surface. Knead by hand for 8 minutes, or until smooth and slightly springy. Rub dough with ½ tablespoon oil. Place in large bowl. Cover tightly with plastic wrap and let dough rise for 1½ hours.
2. Preheat oven to 500°F (260°C). Coat a large ovenproof nonstick pan or pizza pan with cooking spray. Add salt to dough; knead to distribute salt and form dough ball. Press the dough ball into a 14-inch (35 cm) circle on pan.
3. In medium bowl, toss spinach with remaining oil and the lemon juice. Top pizza with spinach and crumbled goat cheese. Bake 10 minutes, or until pizza dough is brown and crisp.
4. Remove from oven. Top with basil, pepper, and garlic powder.

Alternate Grains: Try with other whole-grain flours—or a mixture.

Veal Stew with Millet, Baby Carrots, and Thyme

Makes 6 cups stew and 1½ cups millet. Serves 4.

This is one of the simplest stew recipes you'll find—and it's not only high in protein, but contains 500% of your daily requirements for vitamin A from the carrots. It's also high in B vitamins and minerals.

1½ tablespoons extra-virgin olive oil
1½ pounds (680 g) veal stew meat, cut into cubes
1 large red onion, cut into large dice
½ teaspoon freshly ground black pepper
2 cups reduced-sodium, 99% fat-free beef broth
1 pound (450 g) baby carrots
1 tablespoon finely chopped fresh thyme leaves
½ cup hulled millet
1⅓ cups reduced-sodium vegetable, chicken, or
   beef broth

Nutrition Analysis (1½ cups)
Calories: 370
Calories From Fat: 90
Total Fat: 9g
Saturated Fat: 2.5g
Cholesterol: 90mg
Sodium: 390mg
Carbohydrates: 41g
Dietary Fiber: 4g
Protein: 28g

1. Preheat oven to 350°F (180°C). Heat oil in dutch oven or large ovenproof pot over medium-high heat. Add veal, onions, and pepper. Sauté for 7 minutes or until veal is just cooked through.
2. Mix in beef broth and 2 teaspoons thyme. Bring to simmer. Cover and roast in oven for 30 minutes. Stir in carrots. Cover pot and roast for additional 1½ hours, or until veal is tender. Adjust seasonings.
3. Place small saucepan over medium-high heat. Add millet; stir for 3 minutes, or until millet begins to turn golden brown. Add broth and bring to boil. Reduce to medium-low and cover. Simmer for 18 minutes, or until millet is softened and liquid is absorbed. Remove from heat. Stir in remaining thyme. Let sit covered for 5 minutes.
4. To serve, ladle stew over millet in four shallow soup bowls.

Alternate Grains: Whole-wheat couscous, quinoa, or fine bulgur are ideal alternatives to millet in this stew.

Sweet Tomato-Glazed Veggie Loaf

Makes 1 loaf. Serves 4.

Definitely not your mom's meatloaf. And perhaps more memorable — since there's actually no meat in it at all. Yet this dish is a rich source of B vitamins, especially B_{12}, as well as zinc and iron.

12 oz (340 g) package vegetarian ground beef

1 medium red onion, grated

1 large egg, slightly beaten

1 large egg white, slightly beaten

⅓ cup old-fashioned rolled oats

¼ cup plus 2 tablespoons ketchup

2 teaspoons spicy brown mustard

1 teaspoon finely chopped fresh thyme leaves, plus additional sprigs for garnish, if desired

½ teaspoon garlic powder, or to taste

½ teaspoon freshly ground black pepper

⅛ teaspoon ground cinnamon (optional)

Nutrition Analysis (1 slice)
Calories: 180
Calories From Fat: 15
Total Fat: 2g
Saturated Fat: 0g
Cholesterol: 55mg
Sodium: 730mg
Carbohydrates: 20g
Dietary Fiber: 6g
Protein: 20g

1. Preheat oven to 400°F. (200°C) Combine vegetarian ground beef, onion, egg and egg white, oats, ¼ cup ketchup, mustard, thyme, garlic, pepper, and, if using, cinnamon.
2. On a 9x13-inch (22x32 cm) nonstick baking pan, form meatloaf mixture into loaf shape, about 7x4½-inches (17x11 cm). Brush remaining ketchup over loaf.
3. Bake for 40 minutes, or until cooked through. (Note: Unlike traditional meatloaf, this will still be quite moist when done.) Let sit 10 minutes before slicing.
4. Cut into 4 slices. If desired, garnish with thyme sprigs.

Alternate Grains: Cooked, chilled amaranth or teff is a nice change of pace in place of oats.

Quinoa Stuffed Peppers with Ground Turkey

Makes 4 stuffed peppers. Serves 4.

In need of a rustic comfort food? These stuffed peppers are low in fat and rich in vitamins C and K, iron, zinc, and protein.

¾ cup quinoa

4 large red bell peppers

2 teaspoons extra-virgin olive oil

1 large red onion, chopped

3 large cloves garlic, minced

1½ cups jarred marinara sauce

12 oz (340 g) lean ground turkey breast meat

1 large egg, beaten

⅓ cup chopped fresh parsley

½ teaspoon fine sea salt, or to taste

½ teaspoon ground black pepper, or to taste

**Nutrition Analysis
(1 stuffed pepper)**
Calories: 390
Calories From Fat: 90
Total Fat: 10g
Saturated Fat: 2g
Cholesterol: 85mg
Sodium: 490mg
Carbohydrates: 46g
Dietary Fiber: 8g
Protein: 30g

1. In small saucepan over high heat, bring quinoa and 1½ cups water to boil. Reduce to medium and cover. Cook for 10 minutes. Remove from heat; let sit 5 minutes covered. Move to bowl. Chill.
2. Cut off top inch (2.5 cm) of peppers, discard stem, and dice pepper tops. Scoop out seeds from pepper cavities.
3. Heat oil in nonstick skillet over medium heat. Add peppers, onions, and garlic. Sauté for 8 minutes. Transfer to large bowl. Add quinoa, ½ cup marinara, turkey, egg, parsley, salt, and pepper.
4. Firmly stuff and mound turkey mixture into pepper cavities. Stand peppers in single layer in large, heavy pot. Pour remaining marinara sauce and ½ cup water around peppers and bring to boil.
5. Reduce to medium-low, cover, and simmer 25 minutes. Spoon sauce over each pepper. Cover; cook 20 more minutes, until filling is cooked. Let sit 5 minutes covered. Serve with sauce over peppers.

Alternate Grains: Whole-wheat couscous, wild, and brown rice can be used in place of quinoa for these stuffed peppers.

Shrimp Soba Primavera

Makes 10 cups. Serves 5.

A much more interesting take on the typical pasta primavera. With all of the vegetables in this dish, Shrimp Soba Primavera is loaded with folate, vitamins A, C, and K, as well as potassium and fiber.

12 oz (340 g) soba noodles

2 tablespoons extra-virgin olive oil

4 large garlic cloves, minced

¾ cup unsalted vegetable or chicken broth

2 cups precooked, deveined large shrimp

20 grape tomatoes, halved

2 medium zucchinis, halved vertically, then thinly sliced horizontally

½ cup chopped fresh basil

¼ cup freshly grated Parmigiana-Reggiano cheese

Nutrition Analysis (2 cups)

Calories: 270
Calories From Fat: 50
Total Fat: 6g
Saturated Fat: 1.5g
Cholesterol: 55mg
Sodium: 500mg
Carbohydrates: 41g
Dietary Fiber: 1g
Protein: 16g

1. Cook the soba noodles in large pot of boiling water for 4-5 minutes, or until al dente.
2. Meanwhile, heat oil in large skillet over medium-high heat. Add garlic and sauté for 1 minute. Add broth, cooked shrimp, tomatoes, zucchini, and basil. Simmer for 4–5 minutes, or until zucchini is tender and shrimp is heated through.
3. Drain noodles and return to pot. Add shrimp-vegetable mixture and toss to combine. Add salt to taste.
4. Transfer mixture to bowl; toss or sprinkle with cheese.

Alternate Grains: Using udon noodles or whole-wheat linguine or fettuccine will make this seem like a new dish each time it is prepared. You can also use alternative vegetables.

Louisiana-Style Red Beans and Spelt

Makes about 4½ cups beans and 2 cups spelt.

Serves 6.

No true Louisianan would allow spelt with their red beans. But no true foodie would turn down this clever culinary creation.

1¾ cups small dry red beans, rinsed, soaked in
water in refrigerator overnight, drained
6 cups low-sodium chicken or vegetable broth
¾ cup smoked ham, minced
1 large yellow onion, chopped
1 large green bell pepper, chopped
½ cup chopped fresh Italian parsley
4 large cloves garlic, minced
1 bay leaf
½ teaspoon hot pepper sauce, or to taste
¾ cup spelt
¼ cup finely chopped fresh chives

Nutrition Analysis
(⅓ cup spelt,
¾ cup beans)
Calories: 340
Calories From Fat: 25
Total Fat: 3g
Saturated Fat: 1g
Cholesterol: 55mg
Sodium: 320mg
Carbohydrates: 55g
Dietary Fiber: 15g
Protein: 25g

1. Into large pot add beans, broth, ham, onion, green pepper, ¼ cup parsley, garlic, bay leaves, and hot pepper sauce. Place over medium heat and stir. Cook, uncovered, for 1 hour, stirring occasionally. Cover and cook 30 more minutes, until beans are tender and liquid is absorbed. Remove bay leaf. If necessary, add salt to taste.
2. In medium saucepan over high heat, bring spelt and 3½ cups water to boil; reduce to medium-low and cover. Simmer for 1½ hour or until tender. Remove from heat. Let sit for 10 minutes covered.
3. Serve red beans over spelt. Sprinkle with chives and some parsley.

Alternate Grains: Go more traditional and serve this with brown rice.

Teff Moroccan Chicken Stew

Makes 7 cups. Serves 7.

Tiny grains of teff provide a molasseslike sweetness that balances beautifully with this stew's spices. In just 1 cup, you get 80% of your iron, 50% of your protein, and 25% of your potassium requirements.

2 teaspoons extra-virgin olive oil
4 4-oz (115 g) boneless, skinless chicken breasts
   or thighs
1 Vidalia onion, diced
3 cups reduced-sodium chicken broth
1 cup rinsed, drained, unsalted, canned
   garbanzo beans
1 cup canned, crushed tomatoes
Juice of 1 lemon (3 tablespoons)
1 teaspoon ground cinnamon
½ teaspoon ground cumin
½ teaspoon garlic powder
¾ cup teff
⅓ cup sliced almonds, pan-toasted

Nutrition Analysis (1 cup)
Calories: 380
Calories From Fat: 160
Total Fat: 17g
Saturated Fat: 4g
Cholesterol: 60mg
Sodium: 320mg
Carbohydrates: 32g
Dietary Fiber: 4g
Protein: 25g

1. Heat oil in large pot over medium-high heat. Add chicken; cook for 5 minutes, until brown but not cooked through. Remove to a plate.
2. Add onions to pot over medium heat. Sauté for 5 minutes. Add broth, beans, tomatoes, lemon juice, cinnamon, cumin, and garlic salt. Bring to boil over high heat. Stir in teff. Add chicken.
3. Reduce heat to low and cover. Simmer for 25 minutes or until chicken is cooked through. Remove from heat. Let sit covered for 10 minutes. Adjust seasonings.
4. Divide into serving bowls. Top with almonds.

Alternate Grains: Amaranth will provide a similar texture to this thick, hearty stew.

Side Dishes

Barley with Leeks and Fennel

Makes 5 cups. Serves 6.

*T*his barley recipe is healthy enough to prepare often. The precious spice saffron, takes it to an aromatic level of its own. If you're looking to boost your fiber intake, especially soluble fiber, then this dish is the one.

1 tablespoon canola oil

2 leeks (white and pale green parts only), chopped

1 fennel (anise) bulb, finely chopped

1½ cups whole hull-less barley

4½ cups unsalted, low fat chicken broth

Few threads saffron

¼ cup grated Parmigiana-Reggiano cheese

½ cup chopped fresh basil

1 teaspoon finely chopped fresh thyme leaves

½ teaspoon freshly ground black pepper, or to taste

3 tablespoons pine nuts, pan-toasted

Nutrition Analysis (¾ cup)

Calories: 300
Calories From Fat: 80
Total Fat: 8g
Saturated Fat: 1.5g
Cholesterol: 20mg
Sodium: 180mg
Carbohydrates: 47g
Dietary Fiber: 10g
Protein: 12g

1. Add oil to large pot over medium heat. Once oil is hot, sauté leeks and fennel 8 minutes, or until tender.
2. Stir in barley, broth, and saffron; bring to boil over high heat. Reduce heat to medium-low, cover, and simmer for 55 minutes, or until barley is tender.
3. Stir in cheese, ¾ of the basil, and the thyme. Add pepper to taste.
4. Serve. Top with remaining basil. Sprinkle with pine nuts.

Alternate Grains: Whole-wheat orzo will be wonderful instead of barley. Cooking time and amount of broth will need to be adjusted.

Buckwheat and Bell Pepper-Zucchini Sauté

Makes 8 cups. Serves 8.

*L**ooks like a Greek version of veggie stir-fried rice. It's so moist,
consider molding one-cup portions. All of the peppers in this dish
actually give you 150% of your daily vitamin C requirement.*

1½ cups buckwheat groats

2 tablespoons extra-virgin olive oil

3 cups reduced-sodium vegetable or chicken
   broth

1 large red onion, chopped

2 large cloves garlic, minced

1 large red bell pepper, chopped

1 large yellow bell pepper, chopped

1 medium zucchini, cut vertically, then crosswise
   into slices

1 teaspoon finely chopped fresh oregano

¼ teaspoon fine sea salt, or to taste

½ teaspoon freshly ground black pepper, or to taste

**Nutrition Analysis
(1 cup)**
Calories: 180
Calories From Fat: 40
Total Fat: 4.5g
Saturated Fat: 0.5g
Cholesterol: 0mg
Sodium: 280mg
Carbohydrates: 29g
Dietary Fiber: 4g
Protein: 6g

1. Toast groats in large saucepan over medium-high heat, stirring
   constantly for 4 minutes, or until richly fragrant. Stir in 1
   tablespoon oil. Once groats are coated, carefully add broth; bring
   to boil. Reduce heat to low, cover, and simmer for 10 minutes.
   Remove from heat and keep covered for 10 minutes.
2. Heat remaining oil in large nonstick skillet over medium heat.
   Sauté onion, garlic, and bell peppers for 5 minutes. Add zucchini
   and oregano; sauté 5 more minutes, until vegetables are softened.
3. Stir groats into vegetables in pan until well combined. Add salt and
   pepper to taste. If desired, garnish with oregano leaves.

Alternate Grains: To keep to the Greek theme, enjoy with whole-
wheat couscous, orzo, or bulgur.

Farro Risotto with Tomato and Feta

Makes 4 cups. Serves 6.

In the Mediterranean region, especially Italy, farro has high culinary acclaim. You'll find out why after a taste of this side.

1 cup farro (whole emmer wheat)
2 tablespoons extra-virgin olive oil
¼ cup chopped shallots
½ cup dry red wine
2 cups unsalted chicken or vegetable broth
1 teaspoon unsalted butter
¼ teaspoon freshly ground black pepper,
    or to taste
1 large vine-ripened tomato, seeds removed,
    finely diced
¼ cup crumbled feta cheese

Nutrition Analysis (⅔ cup)
Calories: 170
Calories From Fat: 70
Total Fat: 8g
Saturated Fat: 2g
Cholesterol: 15mg
Sodium: 240mg
Carbohydrates: 19g
Dietary Fiber: 3g
Protein: 6g

1. In large saucepan over high heat bring farro, 1 tablespoon oil, and 6 cups water to boil; reduce heat to medium-low and cover. Simmer for 20 minutes. Drain in mesh strainer.
2. Add remaining oil to medium saucepan over medium heat. Add shallots; sauté 1 minute. Add strained farro and wine. Cook for 3 minutes, or until almost all liquid evaporates, stirring frequently.
3. Increase heat to medium-high. Add 1 cup broth; cook, stirring frequently, for 5 minutes or until liquid is absorbed. Add remaining broth; cook, stirring frequently, for 5 minutes or until liquid is absorbed.
4. Remove from heat. Stir in butter. Add salt and pepper to taste. Fold in tomatoes. Top with feta. If desired, garnish with thinly sliced fresh basil.

Alternate Grains: Whole, hull-less barley will provide a similar farro-like texture to this twist on risotto, but adjust simmering.

Millet Mashers (mock mashed potatoes)

Makes 10 cups. Serves 10.

*S*urprise your dinner guests with this "new-age" style side. It looks a bit like mashed potatoes but has a unique taste of its own and is a lot healthier than white potatoes.

2 teaspoons unsalted butter or trans-free
   margarine
1 teaspoon canola or vegetable oil
Florets of 1 head cauliflower, chopped
1½ cups millet
4 large cloves garlic, peeled
1 teaspoon fine sea salt, or to taste
¼ cup chopped fresh chives

Nutrition Analysis (1 cup)
Calories: 150
Calories From Fat: 25
Total Fat: 2.5g
Saturated Fat: 1g
Cholesterol: 0mg
Sodium: 260mg
Carbohydrates: 27g
Dietary Fiber: 5g
Protein: 5g

1. Add butter or margarine and oil to large saucepan over medium-high heat. Once butter or margarine melts, add cauliflower; sauté for 3 minutes. Add millet; sauté 3 more minutes, or until lightly browned.
2. Carefully add 7 cups water, garlic cloves and salt; bring to boil over high heat. Cover, reduce heat to low, and simmer for 1 hour, or just until no liquid remains.
3. Pour mixture into bowl. Mash with potato masher. Adjust seasonings.
4. Stir in or top with chives.

Alternate Grains: Using amaranth in this recipe will provide a creamier consistency.

Kale with Quinoa and Sesame

Makes 6 cups. Serves 6.

One of the "hottest" ways to get your greens . . . with the "coolest" grain, quinoa. With so much kale, this dish is loaded with antioxidants and vitamins A, C, and K.

2 cups unsalted chicken or vegetable broth

1 cup quinoa

1 large bunch kale, very thinly sliced (thick stems discarded)

1 tablespoon grated fresh ginger

1 large clove garlic, minced

1 tablespoon toasted sesame oil

1 tablespoon rice vinegar

1 tablespoon acacia or orange blossom honey

1½ teaspoons low-sodium soy sauce, or to taste

1 tablespoon toasted sesame seeds

**Nutrition Analysis
(1 cup)**

Calories: 210
Calories From Fat: 50
Total Fat: 6g
Saturated Fat: 1g
Cholesterol: 10mg
Sodium: 180mg
Carbohydrates: 33g
Dietary Fiber: 4g
Protein: 9g

1. Bring broth to boil in dutch oven or large saucepan over high heat. Add quinoa, kale, ginger, and garlic. (Don't stir.) Cover, reduce heat to low. Cook for 15 minutes. Remove from heat. Let sit covered 5 minutes.
2. In small bowl, whisk oil, vinegar, honey, and soy sauce. Drizzle over quinoa-kale mixture. Stir well.
3. Serve hot. Sprinkle with sesame seeds.

Alternate Grains: Whole-wheat couscous or brown rice will both be equally delicious in place of quinoa. Cooking times will need to be adjusted depending on what you choose.

Curried Squash Risotto with Brown and Wild Rice

Makes 4 cups. Serves 6.

While classic risotto is made with Arborio rice, this one uses brown and wild rice. Not only will this have more interesting textures, but with squash, one serving packs your day's worth of vitamin A.

½ of a medium butternut squash, peeled and
   seeded
6½ cups low-sodium chicken broth
1 tablespoon extra-virgin olive oil
1 medium yellow onion, chopped
1 cup long grain brown rice
½ cup wild rice
2 large cloves garlic, minced
1½ teaspoons curry powder
Juice of 1 lime (2 tablespoons), or to taste
4 teaspoons unsalted butter or margarine

Nutrition Analysis (⅔ cup)
Calories: 250
Calories From Fat: 30
Total Fat: 3.5g
Saturated Fat: 0.5g
Cholesterol: 0mg
Sodium: 610mg
Carbohydrates: 46g
Dietary Fiber: 4g
Protein: 9g

1. Halve squash lengthwise. Remove skin with vegetable peeler and remove seeds from only one half. Dice.
2. In large saucepan over medium-low heat, bring broth to simmer.
3. Separately, heat oil in a large pot over medium-high heat. Sauté squash and onion for 8 minutes, or until lightly caramelized. Add brown and wild rice, garlic, and curry powder; cook, stirring, 1 minute. Reduce heat to medium. Carefully stir in ½ cup simmering broth and cook, stirring frequently, until broth is absorbed. Continue simmering and adding broth ½ cup at a time, stirring constantly, making sure each addition is absorbed before adding next. (Note: The risotto will take about 50 minutes.)
4. Stir in lime juice; simmer, stirring, 1 minute. Serve risotto immediately. If desired, top each with a teaspoon pat of butter.

Alternate Grains: Try with all brown rice instead of a mixture of brown and wild rice.

Sorghum, Sweet Bell Pepper, and Pine Nut Pilaf

Makes 4 cups. Serves 6.

A vibrantly colorful side that's quick to fix. Absolutely delicious—hot or cold! Highly nutritious and a great source of vitamin C.

1¼ cups sorghum

1 tablespoon extra-virgin olive oil

1 small or ½ large red onion, finely chopped

½ cup reduced-sodium vegetable or chicken

Juice of 1 small lemon (2 tablespoons)

1 large red or orange bell pepper, finely diced

¼ cup chopped fresh basil

2 tablespoons minced fresh chives

½ teaspoon fine sea salt, or to taste

¼ teaspoon freshly ground black pepper, or to
   taste

¼ cup pine nuts, pan-toasted

Nutrition Analysis (⅔ cup)
Calories: 220
Calories From Fat: 60
Total Fat: 7g
Saturated Fat: 0.5g
Cholesterol: 0mg
Sodium: 240mg
Carbohydrates: 35g
Dietary Fiber: 2g
Protein: 5g

1. In medium saucepan over high heat bring sorghum and 2½ cups water to boil; reduce to medium and cover. Cook for 12 minutes, or until tender. Remove from heat. Let sit for 5 minutes covered.
2. Meanwhile, add oil to large nonstick skillet over medium heat. Once oil is hot, sauté onion for 5 minutes or until softened.
3. Stir in broth, lemon juice, and bell pepper. Continue cooking for 5 minutes. (Note: Some liquid will still remain.)
4. Stir in cooked sorghum. Once sorghum is hot and mixture is well combined, remove from heat.
5. Stir in basil and chives. Sprinkle with pine nuts, salt, and pepper.

Alternate Grains: Prepare with quinoa for an easy substitution.

Spelt Citrus-Pistachio Pilaf

Makes 1¾ cups. Serves 4.

A brilliant pilaf bursting with zesty citrus flavors. Spelt's nutty flavor is complemented by the pistachios, creating a delicious dish rich in vitamin C and riboflavin.

1 teaspoon extra-virgin olive oil

1 teaspoon unsalted butter or margarine

2 large shallots, finely chopped

¾ cup spelt

¼ cup unsalted, shelled pistachios, chopped

1 cup reduced-sodium chicken broth

¼ cup fresh orange juice

Juice of 1 lemon (3 tablespoons juice)

¼ teaspoon fine sea salt, or to taste

⅛ teaspoon white pepper, or to taste

Nutrition Analysis
(½ cup)
Calories: 190
Calories From Fat: 60
Total Fat: 6g
Saturated Fat: 1g
Cholesterol: 5mg
Sodium: 290mg
Carbohydrates: 32g
Dietary Fiber: 1g
Protein: 7g

1. Heat oil and butter in large saucepan over medium heat. Once butter melts, add shallots; sauté for 2 minutes. Add spelt and half of the pistachios; sauté 1 more minute.
2. Increase heat to high. Carefully add 1½ cups water, broth, and juices; bring to boil.
3. Reduce heat to medium-low. Cover and simmer for 1 hour 15 minutes, or until liquid is absorbed and spelt is chewy yet tender. Remove from heat. Let sit covered for 10 minutes.
4. Add salt and pepper to taste. Garnish spelt with some pistachios.

Alternate Grains: You'll particularly enjoy the crunch of the pistachios in this pilaf when using a grain that's softer when cooked, like long-grain brown rice. Cooking time and liquid will need to be adjusted.

Breads & Desserts

Southwestern Cornbread

Make 1 loaf. Serves 20.

Cornbread is a truly American food, particularly of the south. To spice it up, give this Southwest-influenced version an extra kick by adding minced jalapeño peppers to the batter.

½ cup unsalted butter or trans free margarine, melted

1 cup granulated sugar

4 large eggs

¼ cup fat-free evaporated milk

1 10-oz (285 g) package frozen corn, thawed and drained, or 2 cups fresh cooked corn kernels

¾ cup shredded pepper Jack cheese

1 cup unbleached all-purpose flour

1 cup fine yellow cornmeal

1 tablespoon + 1 teaspoon baking powder

½ teaspoon fine sea salt

Nutrition Analysis (1 slice)

Calories: 170
Calories From Fat: 60
Total Fat: 7g
Saturated Fat: 4g
Cholesterol: 60mg
Sodium: 210mg
Carbohydrates: 23g
Dietary Fiber: 1g
Protein: 4g

1. Preheat oven to 300°F (150°C). Lightly coat 9x13-inch (22x32 cm) nonstick baking pan with baking spray.
2. In large bowl, beat melted butter and sugar. Beat in eggs one at a time. Blend in milk, corn, and cheese.
3. In separate bowl, combine cornmeal, flour, baking powder, and salt. Add cornmeal mixture to corn mixture. Blend just until well combined.
4. Pour batter into prepared pan. Bake 1 hour, or until inserted toothpick comes out clean. (Note: The corn kernels will settle to the bottom of the bread during baking.) Remove pan to rack to cool.

Alternate Grains: Consider a mixture of flours such as whole-wheat, millet, amaranth, or buckwheat.

Nutty Millet Banana Bread

Makes 1 loaf—24 thin slices. Serves 24.

Nutritious enough for breakfast; sweet enough for dessert. The millet gives this moist bread a unique, almost candylike crunchiness. This bread is delicious freshly baked or topped with low-sugar jam.

½ cup unsalted butter, melted

1 cup granulated sugar

2 large eggs, well beaten

1 cup unbleached all-purpose flour

¾ cup whole-wheat flour

1 teaspoon baking soda

¼ teaspoon fine sea salt

½ cup hulled millet

4 large fully ripened bananas, mashed

2 teaspoons pure vanilla extract

¼ cup chopped walnuts, toasted

Nutrition Analysis (1 slice)

Calories: 140
Calories From Fat: 45
Total Fat: 5g
Saturated Fat: 2.5g
Cholesterol: 30mg
Sodium: 85mg
Carbohydrates: 23g
Dietary Fiber: 1g
Protein: 2g

1. Preheat oven to 350°F (180°C). In large mixing bowl, cream melted butter and sugar with electric mixer. Add beaten eggs; blend well.
2. In separate bowl, sift flours, baking soda, and salt. Add sifted dry ingredients to butter mixture. Blend on low speed, just until combined.
3. Add millet, mashed bananas, vanilla extract, and nuts to mixture. Stir until just mixed.
4. Coat nonstick loaf pan with baking spray. Pour batter into pan. Bake for 1 hour 10 minutes, or until tester comes out clean. Remove to rack to cool. (Hint: Partially freeze before slicing.)

Alternate Grains: Rolled old-fashioned oats instead of millet will give this bread a smooth, comforting texture.

Soft Rye Bread

Makes 2 loaves—12 slices each; 24 slices total. Serves 24.

Bread the old-fashioned way. No bread machine required. Plus, this recipe has the best of both bread worlds—half rye and half wheat.

3½ cups unbleached all-purpose flour

¼ cup packed dark brown sugar

2 envelopes active dry yeast (½ oz; 14 g)

1 tablespoon whole caraway seeds

1½ teaspoons fine sea salt

1 teaspoon grated orange peel (optional)

2 tablespoons canola or vegetable oil

2 cups dark rye flour

1 egg white

Nutrition Analysis (1 slice)

Calories: 120
Calories From Fat: 15
Total Fat: 1.5g
Saturated Fat: 0g
Cholesterol: 0mg
Sodium: 150mg
Carbohydrates: 23g
Dietary Fiber: 2g
Protein: 3g

1. In large bowl, combine 2 cups all-purpose flour, brown sugar, yeast (not dissolved), 2 teaspoons caraway seeds, salt, and, if using, orange peel. Gradually add 2 cups warm water and oil to flour mixture; beat with electric mixer for 2 minutes at medium speed. Add ½ cup all-purpose flour; beat 2 minutes at high speed. Stir in rye flour and just enough all-purpose flour to make soft dough.
2. Knead on lightly floured surface for 8 minutes, or until elastic. Cover; let rest 10 minutes. Divide dough in half; shape each into loaf. Place on large nonstick baking sheet lightly coated with cooking spray. Cover loosely with cooking spray–coated plastic wrap or foil; let rise in warm, draft-free place for 1 hour, until size doubles.
3. Preheat oven to 400°F (200°C). With knife make 6 slashes atop each loaf. In small bowl, whisk egg white with 1 tablespoon cold water. Brush egg-white mixture over loaves. Sprinkle with some caraway seeds.
4. Bake for 30 minutes or until done. Remove loaves; let cool on rack.

Alternate Grains: Consider a mixture of flours to create multigrain bread. Or, simply go a little heavier on the rye flour.

Bittersweet Buckwheat Chocolate Brownies

Cut into 16 squares. Serves 16.

When it comes to chocolate and health, the bitterer the better. And these brownies fall into that bitter category for sure.

3 3½-oz (100 g) bars high-quality dark (bittersweet) chocolate

¼ cup black cherry or seedless raspberry preserves

¼ cup acacia or orange blossom honey

1 large egg

2 large egg whites

1 teaspoon fine sea salt

pinch of ground cinnamon (optional)

1½ teaspoons pure vanilla extract

½ cup buckwheat flour

¼ cup coarsely chopped almonds (optional)

**Nutrition Analysis
(1 brownie)**
Calories: 130
Calories From Fat: 50
Total Fat: 6g
Saturated Fat: 3g
Cholesterol: 15mg
Sodium: 160mg
Carbohydrates: 21g
Dietary Fiber: 2g
Protein: 3g

1. Preheat oven to 350°F (180°C). Coat 8-inch (20 cm) square nonstick baking pan with cooking spray; set aside.
2. Break chocolate into 1-inch (2.5 cm) pieces; place in medium heatproof bowl. Gently melt chocolate by double boiler. Remove from heat.
3. In large bowl combine preserves, honey, eggs, egg whites, salt, cinnamon (if using), and vanilla extract. Whisk to thoroughly combine. Whisk in flour until smooth. Slowly pour melted chocolate into batter, whisking continuously. Spread batter in pan. If using, sprinkle almonds on top of brownie batter; press with fingers slightly into batter.
4. Bake 22 minutes, or until springy to the touch. Cool on rack. Cut into squares when cool.

Alternate Grains: These brownies will be delicious with nearly any flour. Enjoy experimenting.

Chocolate Peanut Butter Pie

Serves 10.

L*ike a chocolate-covered peanut butter cup, only bigger—and better for you.*

1 package instant fat-free, sugar-free chocolate pudding (1.4 oz; 39 g package)

1½ cups fat-free milk or plain soy milk

¾ cup old-fashioned rolled oats

⅓ cup unbleached all-purpose flour

⅓ cup packed light brown sugar

1 teaspoon natural cocoa powder

¼ teaspoon baking powder

⅛ teaspoon fine sea salt

¼ cup (4 tablespoons) unsalted butter or trans-free margarine, chilled and cut into pieces

½ cup natural, unsalted creamy peanut butter

3 tablespoons acacia or orange blossom honey

**Nutrition Analysis
(1 slice)**
Calories: 230
Calories From Fat: 100
Total Fat: 11g
Saturated Fat: 1.5g
Cholesterol: 0mg
Sodium: 170mg
Carbohydrates: 26g
Dietary Fiber: 2g
Protein: 6g

1. In medium bowl whisk pudding with milk until smooth. Chill.
2. Preheat oven to 350°F (180°C). In another large bowl combine oats, flour, brown sugar, cocoa, baking powder, and salt with fork or pastry blender, breaking up any lumps. Add butter or margarine; blend with pastry blender or with fingers until well combined. Press onto bottom and sides of 9-inch (22 cm) nonstick pie pan.
3. Bake for 12 minutes, or until crisp. Remove and let cool on rack.
4. In large bowl, mix peanut butter and honey till smooth. Stir chilled pudding into peanut-butter mixture until smooth. Pour into cooled pie shell. Refrigerate at least 1 hour before slicing into 10 wedges.

Alternate Grains: Try the crust with buckwheat or other whole-grain flour in place of all-purpose flour for more whole-grain goodness.

Oatmeal Raisin Cookies

Makes 24 cookies. Serves 12.

If you're gonna indulge in a cookie, make it count—nutritionally. These muffinlike cookies are a great source of soluble fiber!

½ cup (8 tablespoons; 1 stick) unsalted
   butter or trans-free margarine, softened

½ cup granulated sugar

1 large egg

⅓ cup natural unsweetened applesauce

¼ cup spiced apple butter

1½ teaspoons pure vanilla extract

¾ cup unbleached all-purpose flour

2 tablespoons raw wheat germ

1 teaspoon baking soda

¼ teaspoon fine sea salt

1 cup old-fashioned rolled oats

⅓ cup raisins

Nutrition Analysis (2 cookies)
Calories: 190
Calories From Fat: 80
Total Fat: 9g
Saturated Fat: 1.5g
Cholesterol: 20mg
Sodium: 160mg
Carbohydrates: 26g
Dietary Fiber: 1g
Protein: 3g

1. Preheat oven to 350°F (180°C). In large bowl, beat butter or margarine and sugar until creamy with electric mixer. Add egg; blend well. Add applesauce, apple butter, and vanilla; blend well.
2. In separate bowl, combine flour, wheat germ, baking soda, and salt. Blend flour mixture into applesauce batter. Stir in oats and raisins.
3. Drop by rounded tablespoon onto parchment paper-lined or nonstick cookie sheets.
4. Bake 12 minutes or until springy to the touch. Cool 1 minute on cookie sheets; remove to rack. Cool completely.

Alternate Grains: Try with a mixture of all-purpose and whole-grain flour of choice to punch up the whole-grain benefits.

Pear Hazelnut Crisp

Serves 6.

A sophisticated version of the rustic crisp classic. Delicious all year round, this dessert works well with peaches and berries too!

4 medium firmly ripe Bosc pears, peeled, cored, and thinly sliced

2 tablespoons firmly packed light brown sugar

1 tablespoon unbleached all-purpose flour

¼ teaspoon ground cinnamon

TOPPING:

½ cup quick or old-fashioned rolled oats, uncooked

¼ cup hazelnuts, pan-toasted, skins rubbed off in kitchen towel, coarsely chopped

2 tablespoons firmly packed light brown sugar

2 tablespoons unsalted butter or trans-free margarine, melted

⅛ teaspoon ground cinnamon

Nutrition Analysis (1 slice)
Calories: 180
Calories From Fat: 70
Total Fat: 7g
Saturated Fat: 1g
Cholesterol: 0mg
Sodium: 0mg
Carbohydrates: 29g
Dietary Fiber: 4g
Protein: 2g

1. Preheat oven to 400°F (200°C). In large bowl, combine pears and 3 tablespoons water. Add brown sugar, flour, and cinnamon; stir until pear slices are evenly coated.
2. Pour into 8-inch (20 cm) round nonstick baking pan.
3. In medium bowl, stir oats, chopped hazelnuts, brown sugar, melted butter, and cinnamon until well mixed. Sprinkle evenly over pears.
4. Bake 20 minutes, or until pears are tender and topping is crisp. Scoop to serve. Serve while warm. If desired, enjoy with vanilla frozen yogurt.

Alternate Grains: Add a sprinkle of wheat germ to the topping mixture for an extra crunch.

Brown Rice Pudding

Makes 4 cups. Serves 6.

Pudding that's full of flavor—and nutrition. Now that's sweet. Serve with fat-free whipped topping for a healthy dessert.

1 cup long grain brown rice

1 cup evaporated fat free milk

1 large egg

2 large egg whites

⅓ cup unsweetened apple juice

3 tablespoons firmly packed light brown sugar

1 teaspoon pure vanilla extract

¼ cup raisins

1 cinnamon stick

⅛ teaspoon ground cinnamon

Nutrition Analysis
(⅔ cup)
Calories: 220
Calories From Fat: 15
Total Fat: 2g
Saturated Fat: 0g
Cholesterol: 35mg
Sodium: 80mg
Carbohydrates: 42g
Dietary Fiber: 1g
Protein: 8g

1. In small saucepan over high heat, combine rice with 2¼ cups water. Bring to boil. Cover and reduce heat to low. Simmer for 55 minutes, or until liquid is absorbed. Remove from heat. Let sit covered for 5 to 10 minutes.
2. In medium saucepan whisk evaporated milk, egg, egg whites, juice, brown sugar, and vanilla extract. Stir in raisins, cinnamon stick, and warm, cooked rice. Place over medium-low heat. Cook, stirring constantly, for 8 minutes, or until thickened.
3. Remove cinnamon stick. Transfer pudding to a 6 small bowls or ramekins. Cover each with wax paper. Chill for at least 1 hour. Sprinkle each serving with ground cinnamon.

Alternate Grains: Prepare this comfort food with other types of rice or a rice mixture.

Eating Out and Ordering In

Unlike foods you buy in your local supermarket, restaurant and take-out meals don't usually come with a list of ingredients, so it can be hard to know exactly what you're getting. But even when specific ingredients aren't available, a few strategies can help you find whole-grain choices when eating out. When eating in restaurants, try the following:

Start the day right. If you love to go out for Sunday brunch, or you eat out for breakfast when you travel, take advantage of all the great whole-grain choices that are available at breakfast. The best choice, of course, is oatmeal. Ask for low-fat milk, and raisins rather than sugar, for a delicious and filling breakfast. Also, ask for whole-wheat dry toast (no butter), whole-grain muffins, cereals, or whole-wheat or buckwheat pancakes. Better to use small amounts of jams or syrups instead of added fat to save calories. And watch out for oat-bran muffins from a bakery, as they can pack anywhere from 500 to 800 calories per muffin. Remember, just because bakery products may have a big sign displaying that everything is made with "trans-free fats," this doesn't mean it is calorie-free. You still need to be careful and eat small amounts if you are craving baked goods.

Look to the sides. While meat, chicken, or fish generally plays the starring role on most North Americans' plates, side dishes are the way to go if you want to get more whole grains when eating out. Restaurants are now offering a wider variety of interesting and healthful grain-based sides. Try quinoa, barley pilaf, wild rice, or tabbouleh, which is made with bulgar wheat, or side dishes with buckwheat groats such as kasha or bowties. Even corn on the cob or fish with a cornmeal crust would be excellent choices. Brown rice risotto is also a delicious way to add whole grains to your diet.

Go Asian. Asian restaurants frequently offer lots of whole-grain options. At Chinese or Thai restaurants, always ask for brown rice instead of the traditional white rice. Or, if you're at a Japanese restaurant, order buckwheat soba noodles and ask them to make your sushi or rolls with brown rice instead of white rice.

Sip some soup. Soups are another good way to sneak some extra grains into your meal. Look for ones made with barley or wild rice and lots of vegetables. For an added bonus, skip the oyster crackers and bring your own whole-grain spelt, rice, or wheat crackers from home.

Think vegetarian. Even if you're not a vegetarian, consider choosing the vegetarian entrée when eating out. These dishes often incorporate grains such as brown rice, quinoa, and millet in a creative and tasty way and offer choices not found elsewhere on the menu.

Choose bread wisely. More restaurants are offering a selection of whole-wheat, whole-grain, rye, and pumpernickel breads. So, when given the choice between these and sourdough, white, or even foccacia, go for the grain. And skip the butter—it's always best to request olive oil for dipping, which is a great source of monounsaturated fats.

Getting Grains on the Run or at Take-out Meals

Beat the morning (sugar) rush. If you typically grab coffee and a donut, muffin, or bagel on the way to work, try substituting a protein bar. Look for those with at least 7 grams of protein, some fiber, and not more than 200 calories. Whole-grain breakfast bars are starting to be readily available in convenience stores where coffee is sold. Prepare our oat-bran banana walnut muffin recipe in advance (see page 154) and grab one for breakfast in the morning on the way to work or when you take the kids to school. Keep them in the freezer at home as well, and they can defrost while you are traveling.

Branch out. Try your local supermarket deli or salad bar for selections made with wheat berries, bulgar or whole-wheat noodles. Upscale gourmet delis have lots of interesting choices, and may serve whole grains every day upon request. You can also bring in leftover grain recipes from home and keep them in the refrigerator or freezer at the office. This not only saves time but also money. Remember to pick up disposable storage containers next time you are at the market.

Send in the subs. These days, even many chain delis and sub shops offer whole-wheat rolls, breads, and even whole-wheat pizza as options. And, pass on the potato chips and grab some whole-grain pita chips.

Watch portions. Eating out can be too much of a good thing. Be sure to keep portions in check when serving yourself from the salad bar or ordering deli sandwiches. If a whole sub seems overwhelming, eat half or share with a friend or colleague from work. About 1 cup cooked grains would be considered two servings, so add a few tablespoons of several different grains to top your fresh baby spinach or field greens salad. Since most of these salads already have dressing mixed in, skip the added dressing to save calories.

Don't be afraid to ask. If you frequently get take-out from establishments where whole grains are not available, don't be afraid to ask them to offer these selections. These days, restaurants and eateries are becoming just as health-conscious as consumers, so it is common practice to try to meet consumer demands. For example, Chinese take-out places could easily serve brown rice if requested.

Whole-Grain Resources

Grain Organizations

Agriculture and Agri-food Canada
www.agr.gc.ca

Bell Institute of Health and Nutrition
www.bellinstitute.com

Dieticians of Canada
www.dieticians.ca

Health Canada
www.hc-sc.gc.ca

National Barley Foods Council
www.barleyfoods.org

Old Ways Preservation Trust
www.oldwayspt.org

United States Department
of Agriculture
www.usda.gov

USA Rice Association
www.usarice.com

USDA Food Guide Pyramid
www.MyPyramid.gov

Wheat Food Council
www.wheatfoods.org

Whole Grain Council
www.wholegraincouncil.org

Whole Grain Health: A Global Summit
www.wholegrain.umn.edu

Whole Grains Bureau
www.wholegrainsbureau.ca

Grain Products

Annie's Organic Foods
www.annies.com

Arrowhead Mills Consumer Relations
www.arrowheadmill.com

Back To Nature Foods
www.backtonaturefoods.com

The Baker
www.the-baker.com

Barbara's Bakery
www.barbarasbakery.com

Barilla America
www.barillaus.com

Berlin Natural Bakery
www.speltbread.com

Bob's Red Mill
www.bobsredmill.com

Carolina® Rice
www.carolinarice.com

Dr. Kracker
www.drkracker.com

Earth's Best
www.earthsbest.com

Eden Organic
www.edenfoods.com

General Mills Inc.
www.wholegrainlife.com

Great Harvest Bread Company
www.greatharvestsea.com

Health Valley
www.healthvalley.com

Hodgson Mill
www.hodgsonmill.com

Indian Harvest
www.indianharvest.com

Kashi Company
www.kashi.com

Kellogg's
www.kelloggs.com/us

King Arthur Flour
www.kingarthur.com

Kraft Foods
www.kraftfoods.com

Mosher Products
www.wheatandgrain.com

Nature Bake
www.naturebake.com

Nature's Path Organic
www.naturespath.com

Pacific Bakery: Yeast-Free
www.pacificbakery.com

Post Whole Grain Cereals
www.kraftfoods.com/postcereals

Quaker Oats Company
www.quakeroatmeal.com

Quinoa Corporation
www.quinoa.net

Rudi's Organic Bakery
www.rudisbakery.com

RyVita Crackers
www.ryvita.com

Sunnyland Mills
www.sunnylandmills.com

SunWest Foods Inc.
www.sunwestfoods.com

Supreme Rice
www.supremerice.com

Teff Compnay
www.teffco.com

Tumaro's Gourmet Tortillas
www.tumaros.com

Uncle Ben's Rice
www.unclebens.com

Vita-Spelt Products
www.purityfoods.com

Wasa Crackers
www.wasa-usa.com

Whole Foods Markets
www.wholefoodsmarket.com

Resources and Products for a Gluten-Free Lifestyle

Canadian Celiac Association
www.celiac.ca

Celiac Disease Foundation
www.celiac.org

Celiac Sprue Association
www.csaceliacs.org

Gluten Intolerance Group
of North America
www.gluten.net

The National Foundation for
Celiac Awareness
www.celiacawareness.org

Authentic Foods
www.authenticfoods.com

Cherry Brook Kitchen
www.cherrybrookkitchen.com

DeBoles
www.deboles.com

Eden Foods Inc.
www.edenfoods.com

Ener-G Foods
www.ener-g.com

Enjoy Life Natural Brands
www.Enjoylifenb.com

Gabriele Macaroni Products
www.gabrielepasta.com

Glutino
www.glutino.com

Gluten-Free Pantry
www.glutenfree.com

Nu-World Amaranth
www.nuworldamaranth.com

Mary's Gone Crackers
www.marysgonecrackers.com

Pamela's Products
www.pamelasproducts.com

Perky's 100% Natural
www.perkysnaturalfoods.com

Special Foods
www.specialfoods.com

Westbrae Natural
www.westbrae.com

References

Weight Loss References

Barton BA, Eldridge AL, Thompson D, Affenito SG, Striegel-Moore RH, Franko DL, Albertson AM, Crockett SJ. The relationship of breakfast and cereal consumption to nutrient intake and body mass index: the National Heart, Lung, and Blood Institute Growth and Health Study. *J Am Diet Assoc.* 2005;105(9):1383-9.

Bazzano LA, Song Y, Bubes V, Good CK, Manson JE, Liu S. Dietary intake of whole and refined grain breakfast cereals and weight gain in men. *Obesity Research.* 2005;13(11):1952-1960.

Edge MS, Jones JM, Marquart L. A new life for whole grains. *J Am Diet Assoc.* 2005;105(12):1856-60.

Koh-Banerjee P et al. Changes in whole grain, bran, and cereal fiber consumption in relation to 8-y weight gain among men. *Am J Clin Nutr.* 2004;80: 1237-45.

Liu S, Willett WC, Manson JE, Hu FB, Rosner B, Colditz G. Relation between changes in intakes of dietary fiber and grain products and changes in weight and development of obesity among middle-aged women. *Am J Clin Nutr.* 2003;78(5):920-7.

Rampersaud GC et al. Breakfast habits, nutritional status, body weight, and academic performance in children and adolescents. *J Am Diet Assoc.* 2005; 105:743-60.

Slavin JL. Dietary fiber and body weight. *Nutrition.* 2005;21(3):411-8.

Song WO, Chun OK, Obayashi S, Cho S, Chung CE. Is consumption of breakfast associated with body mass index in US adults? *J Am Diet Assoc.* 2005; 105(9):1373-82.

Steffen LM, Jacobs DR Jr, Murtaugh MA, Moran A, Steinberger J, Hong CP, Sinaiko AR. Whole grain intake is associated with lower body mass index and greater insulin sensitivity among adolescents. *Am J Epid.* 2003;12:573-7.

Yao M, Roberts SB. Dietary energy density and weight regulation. *Nutrition Reviews.* 2001;59:247-58.

Heart Disease and Metabolic Syndrome References

Alberti KG. Zimmet P. Shaw J. IDF Epidemiology Task Force Consensus Group. The metabolic syndrome—a new worldwide definition. *Lancet.* 2005; 366(9491): 1059-62.

Anderson JW. Diet first, then medication for hypercholesterolemia. *JAMA*. 2003; 290(4): 531-533.

Anderson JW, Hanna TH, Peng X, Kryscio RJ. Whole grain foods and heart disease Risk. *J Am Coll of Nutr*. 2000;19(No.3):291S-299S.

Anderson, JW. Whole grains and coronary heart disease: the whole kernel of truth. *Am J Clin Nutr*. 2004;80:1459-60.

Deen D, Pi Sunyer X. Chapter 7: Metabolic Syndrome in Carson JS, Burke F, Hark L. eds. *Cardiovascular Nutrition Strategies and Tools for Disease Management and Prevention* 2nd Edition. *American Dietetic Association*. 2005.

Deen D. Metabolic Syndrome: A Time for Action. *American Family Physician*. 2004;69:2875-82.

He J, Klag MJ, Whelton PK, Mo JP, Chen JY, Qian MC, Mo PS, He GQ. Oats and buckwheat intakes and cardiovascular disease risk factors in an ethnic minority of China. *Am J Clin Nutr*. 1995;61(2):366-72.

Hu FB, Willett WC. Optimal diets for prevention of coronary heart disease. *JAMA*. 2002;288(20): 2569-2578.

Jacobs Jr DR, Meyer KA, Kushi LH, Folsom AR. Is whole grain intake associated with reduced total and cause-specific death rates in older women? The Iowa Women's Health Study. *Am J Public Health*. 1999; 89(3):322-329.

Jacobs DR Jr, Gallaher DD. Whole grain intake and cardiovascular disease: a review. *Curr Atheroscler Rep*. 2004;6(6):415-23.

Jenkins DJ, Kendall CW, Marchie A, Faulkner DA, Wong JM, de Souza R, Emam A, Parker TL, Vidgen E, Lapsley KG, Trautwein EA, Josse RG, Leiter LA, Connelly PW. Effects of a dietary portfolio of cholesterol-lowering foods vs. lovastatin on serum lipids and C-reactive protein. *JAMA*. 2003;290(4):502-510.

Jensen MK, Koh-Banerjee P, Hu FB, Franz M, Sampson L, Gronbaek M, Rimm EB. Intakes of whole grains, bran, and germ and the risk of coronary heart disease in men. *Am J Clin Nutr*. 2004;80:1492-9.

Liu S, Manson JE, Stampfer MJ, Rexrode KM, Hu FB, Rimm EB, Willett WC. Whole grain consumption and risk of ischemic stroke in women: A prospective study. *JAMA*. 2000;284(12):1534-40.

Liu S, Stampfer MJ, Hu FB, Giovannucci E, Rimm E, Manson JE, Hennekens CH, Willett WC. Whole-grain consumption and risk of coronary heart disease: results from the Nurses' Health Study. *Am J Clin Nutr*. 1999;70(3):412-9.

Rimm EB, Ascherio A, Giovannucci D, Spiegelman D, Stampfer MJ, Willet WC. Vegetable, fruit, and cereal fiber intake and risk of coronary heart disease among men. *JAMA*. 1996;275(6):447-51.

Saely CH, Aczel S, Marte T, Langer P, Hoefle G, Drexel H. The metabolic syndrome, insulin resistance, and cardiovascular risk in diabetic and nondiabetic patients. *J ClinEndocrin Metab.* 2005;90(10):5698-703.

Slavin J. Whole grains and human health. *Nurt Res Rev.* 2004; 17:99-110

Steffen LM, Jacobs DR Jr, Stevens J, Shahar E, Carithers T, Folsom AR. Associations of whole-grain, refined-grain, and fruit and vegetable consumption with risks of all-cause mortality and incident coronary artery disease and ischemic stroke: the Atherosclerosis Risk in Communities (ARIC) Study. *Am J Clin Nutr.* 2003;78(3):383-90.

Stone NJ, Saxon D. Approach to treatment of the patient with metabolic syndrome: lifestyle therapy. *Am J Cardiology.* 2005;96(4A):15E-21E.

Trowell, H. Dietary fiber, ischemic heart disease and diabetes mellitus. *Proc Nutr Soc.* 1973;32:151-157.

Diabetes References

Anderson JW. Randles KM. Kendall CW. Jenkins DJ. Carbohydrate and fiber recommendations for individuals with diabetes: a quantitative assessment and meta-analysis of the evidence. *J Am College Nutrition.* 2004; 23(1):5-17.

Fung TT, Schulze M, Manson JE, Willett WC, Hu FB. Dietary patterns, meat intake and the risk of type 2 diabetes in women. *Arch Intern Med.* 2004;164(20):2235-40.

Fung TT, Hu FB, Pereira MA, Liu S, Stampfer MJ, Colditz GA, Willett WC. Whole-grain intake and the risk of type 2 diabetes: a prospective study in men. *Am J Clin Nutr.* 2002;76(3):535-40.

Jenkins DJ, Kendall CW, Augustin LS, Martini MC, Axelsen M, Faulkner D, Vidgen E, Parker T, Lau H, Connelly PW, Teitel J, Singer W, Vandenbroucke AC, Leiter LA, Josse RG. Effect of wheat bran on glycemic control and risk factors for cardiovascular disease in type 2 diabetes. *Diabetes Care.* 2002;25(9):1522-8.

Juntunen KS, Laaksonen DE, Poutanen KS, Niskanen LK, Mykkanen HM. High-fiber rye bread and insulin secretion and sensitivity in healthy postmenopausal women. *Am J Clin Nutr.* 2003;77(2):385-91.

Kabir M. Oppert JM. Vidal H. Bruzzo F. Fiquet C. Wursch P. Slama G. Rizkalla SW. Four-week low-glycemic index breakfast with a modest amount of soluble fibers in type 2 diabetic men. *Metabolism: Clinical & Experimental.* 2002;51(7):819-26.

Kelley DE.Sugars and starch in the nutritional management of diabetes mellitus. *Am J Clin Nutr.* 2003;78(4):858S-864S.

Lang R, Jebb SA.Who consumes whole grains, and how much? *Proc Nutr Soc.* 2003;62(1):123-7.

Liese AD, Roach AK, Sparks KC, Marquart L, D'Agostino RB Jr, Mayer-Davis EJ. Whole-grain intake and insulin sensitivity: the Insulin Resistance Atherosclerosis Study. *Am J Clin Nutr.* 2003;78(5):965-71.

Liu S. Whole-grain foods, dietary fiber, and type 2 diabetes: searching for a kernel of truth. *Am J Clin Nutr.* 2003;77(3):527-9.

Liu S. Intake of refined carbohydrates and whole grain foods in relation to risk of type 2 diabetes mellitus and coronary heart disease. *J Am Coll Nutr.* 2002;21(4):298-306.

Lopez-Ridaura R, Willett WC, Rimm EB, Liu S, Stampfer MJ, Manson JE, Hu FB. Magnesium intake and risk of type 2 diabetes in men and women. *Diabetes Care.* 2004;27(1):134-40.

McKeown NM, Meigs JB, Liu S, Saltzman E, Wilson PW, Jacques PF. Carbohydrate nutrition, insulin resistance, and the prevalence of the metabolic syndrome in the Framingham Offspring Cohort. *Diabetes Care.* 2004;78:965-71.

McKeown NM. Whole grain intake and insulin sensitivity: evidence from observational studies. *Nutr Rev.* 2004;62(7 Pt 1):286-91.

McKeown NM, Meigs JB, Liu S, Wilson PW, Jacques PF. Whole-grain intake is favorably associated with metabolic risk factors for type 2 diabetes and cardiovascular disease in the Framingham Offspring Study. *Am J Clin Nutr.* 2002;76(2):390-8.

Montonen J, Knekt P, Jarvinen R, Aromaa A, Reunanen A. Whole-grain and fiber intake and the incidence of type 2 diabetes. *Am J Clin Nutr.* 2003;77(3): 622-9.

Murtaugh MA, Jacobs DR Jr, Jacob B, Steffen LM, Marquart L. Epidemiological support for the protection of whole grains against diabetes. *Proc Nutr Soc.* 2003;62(1):143-9.

Pereira MA, Jacobs DR Jr, Pins JJ, Raatz SK, Gross MD, Slavin JL, Seaquist ER. Effect of whole grains on insulin sensitivity in overweight hyperinsulinemic adults. *Am J Clin Nutr.* 2002;75(5):848-55.

Rendell M, Vanderhoof J, Venn M, Shehan MA, Arndt E, Rao CS, Gill G, Newman RK, Newman CW. Effect of a barley breakfast cereal on blood glucose and insulin response in normal and diabetic patients. *Plant Foods Hum Nutr.* 2005;60(2):63-7.

Schulze MB, Hu FB. Primary prevention of diabetes: what can be done and how much can be prevented? *Annual Rev Public Health.* 2005;26:445-67.

Schwenke DC. Insulin resistance, low-fat diets, and low-carbohydrate diets: time to test new menus. *Curr Opin Lipidol.* 2005;16(1):55-60.

Venn BJ, Mann JI. Cereal grains, legumes and diabetes. *Eur J Clin Nutr.* 2004; 58(11):1443-61.

Wolever TM, Campbell JE, Geleva D, Anderson GH. High-fiber cereal reduces postprandial insulin responses in hyperinsulinemic but not normoinsulinemic subjects. *Diabetes Care.* 2004;27(6):1281-5.

214

Cancer References

Calle EE, Rodriguez C, Walker-Thurmond K, Thun MJ. Overweight, obesity and mortality from cancer in a prospectively studied cohort of U.S. adults. *New Eng J Medicine.* 2003;348:1625-38.

Hill MJ.Nutrition and human cancer. *Ann N Y Acad Sci.* 1997;833:68-78.

Jacobs DR Jr, Marquart L, Slavin J, Kushi LH. Whole-grain intake and cancer: an expanded review and meta-analysis. *Nutr Cancer.* 1998;30(2):85-96

Kasum CM, Nicodemus K, Harnack LJ, Jacobs DR Jr, Folsom AR; Iowa Women's Health Study. Whole grain intake and incident endometrial cancer: the Iowa Women's Health Study. *Nutr Cancer.* 2001;39(2):180-6.

La Vecchia C, Chatenoud L, Negri E, Franceschi S. Whole cereal grains, fibre and human cancer. Whole grain cereals and cancer in Italy. *Proc Nutr Soc.* 2003;62(1):45-9.

Larsson SC, Giovannucci E, Bergkvist L, Wolk A. Whole grain consumption and risk of colorectal cancer: a population-based cohort of 60,000 women.*Br J Cancer.* 2005;92(9):1803-7.

McCullough ML, Robertson AS, Chao A, Jacobs EJ, Stampfer MJ, Jacobs DR, Diver WR, Calle EE, Thun MJ.A prospective study of whole grains, fruits, vegetables and colon cancer risk. *Cancer Causes Control.* 2003;14(10):959-70.

van Rensburg SJ. Epidemiologic and dietary evidence for a specific nutritional predisposition to esophageal cancer.*J National Cancer Institute.* 1981; 67:243-51.

Williams MT, Hord NG.The role of dietary factors in cancer prevention: beyond fruits and vegetables. *Nutr Clin Pract.* 2005;20(4):451-9.

Gastrointestinal and Celiac Disease References

Burkitt D. A deficiency of dietary fiber may be one cause of certain colonic and venous disorders. *Am J Digestive Disorders.* 1976;21(2):104-8.

Burkitt D. Fiber as protective against gastrointestinal disorders. *Am J Gastroenterology.* 1984; 79(4):249-52.

Chand N, Mihas AA. Celiac Disease: Current concepts in diagnosis and treatment. *Clin Gastroenterology.* 2006;40(1):3-14.

Cremonini F, Talley NJ. Diagnostic and therapeutic strategies in the irritable bowel syndrome. *Minerva Med.* 2004;95(5):427-41.

Floch MH. Use of diet and probiotic therapy in the irritable bowel syndrome: analysis of the literature.*J Clin Gastroenterology.* 2005;39(4 Suppl 3):S243-6.

Frizelle F, Barclay M. Constipation in adults. *Clinical Evidence.* 2004;(12):610-22.

Hsieh C. Treatment of constipation in older adults. *American Family Physician.* 2005;72(11):2277-84.

Hyams JS. Diet and gastrointestinal disease. *Current Opinion Pediatrics.* 2002; 14(5):567-9.

Kupper C. Dietary guidelines and implementation for celiac disease. *Gastroenterology.* 2005;128(4 Suppl 1):S121-7.

Lea R, Whorwell PJ. The role of food intolerance in irritable bowel syndrome. *Gastroenterology Clin North Am.* 2005;34(2):247-55.

Marlett JA, McBurney MI, Slavin JL; American Dietetic Association. Position of the American Dietetic Association: health implications of dietary fiber. *J Am Diet Assoc.* 2002;102(7):993-1000.

Storsrud S, Hulthen LR, Lenner RA. Beneficial effects of oats in the gluten-free diet of adults with special reference to nutrient status, symptoms and subjective experiences. *British J Nutrition.* 2003;90(1):101-7.

Schwesinger WH, Kurtin WE, Page CP, Stewart RM, Johnson R. Soluble dietary fiber protects against cholesterol gallstone formation. *Am J Surg.* 1999;177(4):307-10.

Thompson T, Dennis M, Higgins LA, Lee AR, Sharrett MK. Gluten-free diet survey: are Americans with celiac disease consuming recommended amounts of fiber, iron, calcium and grain foods? *J Hum Nutr Diet.* 2005;18(3):163-9.

Tillisch K, Chang L. Diagnosis and treatment of irritable bowel syndrome: state of the art. *Curr Gastroenterol Rep.* 2005;7(4):249-56.

Torii A, Toda G. Management of irritable bowel syndrome. *Internal Medicine.* 2004;43(5):353-9.

Tsai CJ, Leitzmann MF, Willett WC, Giovannucci EL. Long-term intake of dietary fiber and decreased risk of cholecystectomy in women. *Am J Gastroenterology.* 2004;99(7):1364-70.

Index

Acknowledgments

First and foremost, we would like to thank DK for helping us make *The Whole Grain Diet Miracle* a reality; Carl Raymond, Therese Burke, Anja Schmidt, Timothy Shaner, Dirk Kaufman, Sharon Lucas, and Rachel Kempster.

A special thank you to Jackie Neugent, RD, CDN, Culinary and Nutrition Communication Consultant in New York City, who developed and tested all 50 recipes. We could not have done this book without her and very much appreciate her skillful work and delicious recipes.

This book would not have been possible without the tireless efforts of the University of Pennsylvania students: Galina Movshovich, Elizabeth Horvitz, and Tracey Liebman. They have all completed an extensive amount of research, writing, editing, and recipe analysis, and we are very grateful for their assistance. Jeremy Brauer, University of Pennsylvania School of Medicine fourth-year student also deserves a great deal of credit for completing the extensive literature reviews and analysis of the 80 research studies that we report in Chapter 1.

Thank you to Jamie Spencer, professional health and science writer, for contributing lots of great ideas for the "Transitioning to Whole Grains," "Getting Kids to Eat More Whole Grains," and "Finding Whole Grains When Eating Out" sections.

We would also like to thank the BBC New York Production Company, TLC, and Discovery Channel for selecting Dr. Lisa Hark to host the "Honey We're Killing the Kids" show. The BBC team has become our family and has been top notch in all aspects of production.

Finally, to our agent, Beth Shepard, who was so excited about this project, she jumped right in to make it happen. For believing in us, listening so well, and always being there with support and encouragement, we thank you so very much.

Photo Credits